GEOMETRY

THE LANGUAGE OF SPACE AND FORM

THE HISTORY OF MATHEMATICS

GEOMETRY

THE LANGUAGE OF SPACE AND FORM

John Tabak, Ph.D.

☑®
Facts On File, Inc.

GEOMETRY: The Language of Space and Form

Copyright © 2004 by John Tabak, Ph.D.
Permissions appear after relevant quoted material.

Facts On File, Inc.
132 West 31st Street
New York NY 10001

Library of Congress Cataloging-in-Publication Data

Tabak, John.
    Geometry: the language of space and form/John Tabak.
        p. cm. — (History of mathematics)
    Includes bibliographical references and index.
    ISBN 0-8160-4953-X (hardcover)
    1. Geometry—History. I. Title
    QA443.5.T33 2004
    516—dc222003017340

Text design by David Strelecky
Cover design by Kelly Parr
Illustrations by Patricia Meschino

Printed in the United States of America

MP FOF 10 9 8 7 6 5 4 3 2 1

This book is printed on acid-free paper.

To Oliver Clifton Blaylock, friend and mentor.

CONTENTS

ACKNOWLEDGMENTS

The author is deeply appreciative of Frank Darmstadt, Executive Editor, for his many helpful suggestions and of Dorothy Cummings, Project Editor, for the insightful work that she did editing this volume.

Special thanks to Penelope Pillsbury and the staff of the Brownell Library, Essex Junction, Vermont, for their extraordinary help with the many difficult research questions that arose during the preparation of this book.

INTRODUCTION

What is geometry? What is it that we learn when we learn geometry?

Points, lines, and surfaces are some of the things that mathematicians study when they study geometry, but human beings have always been interested in questions of line and form. Cave paintings from Lascaux, France, made during the last ice age show remarkably sophisticated pictures of wild animals. These beautiful images were created about 15,000 years ago. In the history of humankind they are almost unimaginably old. Humans were hunting mammoths when these pictures were painted. It was the Stone Age. There was no written language anywhere in the world until thousands of years after these images were completed, and yet these cave paintings show that 15,000 years ago cave artists were wonderfully sensitive in their use of line and form. Does this mean that they knew geometry? And if they did know some geometry, what part of the mathematical subject of geometry did they know?

For centuries European, Middle Eastern, and North African mathematicians believed that they knew the answer to the question of what constitutes geometry. For them the answer was easy. The term *geometry* meant the geometry of the ancient Greeks. This type of geometry is called Euclidean geometry after one of the best known of all Greek mathematicians, Euclid of Alexandria. The answer to the question, What is it that we learn when we learn geometry? was (to them) equally obvious: We learn the theorems and proofs in Euclid's most famous work, *Elements*. These early mathematicians did not question whether other geometries might exist. It was their belief that most of the geometry that could be learned had already been learned elsewhere at an earlier time and that all that was left for them to do were to master the geometry of the Greeks and to clarify what they saw as those few points remaining in Greek geometry that still needed clarification.

Euclidean geometry *was* geometry. All of nature, they believed, was an exercise in Euclidean geometry.

That the ancient Greeks made tremendous advances in geometry is common knowledge. For almost a thousand years Greek culture produced generation after generation of outstanding mathematicians. It is a record of mathematical excellence and longevity that no other culture has matched—either before or since. Beginning almost from scratch, the Greeks asked profound questions about the nature of mathematics and what it means to understand mathematics. They created the idea of proof, and they worked hard to place geometry on a firm logical foundation. Many Greek mathematical discoveries—the proofs as well as the statements of the results themselves—still sound modern to today's reader. The Greeks invented mathematics in the sense that we now understand the term, but their work offers little insight into contemporary mathematicians' current understanding of geometry. Today mathematicians recognize that Euclidean geometry is simply one geometry among many.

A more modern definition of geometry is that it is the study of geometric properties. That is the short, easy answer. But it is clearly an incomplete answer. It simply shifts our attention away from the word *geometry* and toward the phrase *geometric properties.*

What are geometric properties? Points, lines, planes, angles, curves, surfaces, and bodies in three (and even more!) dimensions may all be worthy of geometric study, but not every property of an object is a geometric property. The shape of a triangle may be considered a geometric property, but its color, its temperature, and its distance from the reader are all examples of properties that are not geometric. Perhaps that is obvious, but it is also important. The key to understanding what mathematicians study when they study geometry lies in recognizing which properties of an object are geometric.

For example, imagine a triangle on a flat surface with the property that all three of its sides are the same length. (A triangle with three equal sides is called an equilateral triangle.) It is not difficult to prove that because our triangle has three equal sides it must also have three equal angles. That it has three equal angles is a *conse-*

quence of the fact that it has three equal sides. We can go further: Because the three angles within our triangle are equal, the measure of each angle must be 60°. So knowing that all three sides of our triangle are the same length allows us to deduce that all angles within our triangle are 60° angles.

Now suppose that we tilt our triangle out of its original position. Is it still an equilateral triangle? Are all of its angles still of equal measure? Does each angle still measure 60°? Can we be sure, or do we have to reinvestigate our triangle each time we tilt it or move it a little off to the side?

Most of us would simply assume that once we discover the measures of the angles of a triangle we should not have to reestablish our discoveries just because we moved our triangle out of its original position. Euclid made the same assumption. Tilting or sliding the triangle from one position to the next should not change the length of the sides or the measures of the angles. Perhaps this is obvious to you. Less obvious, perhaps, is that this simple example also contains the key to understanding what it is that mathematicians study when they study geometry.

Geometry is the study of just those properties of a figure that *do not* change under a particular set of motions. Euclidean geometry, for example, is the study of those properties of a figure that do not change when the figure is tilted (rotated) or when it is moved along a straight line (translated). When the ancient Greeks proved that some figure had a particular geometric property, the proof also applied to *every* figure, located anywhere, that could, through a series of translations and rotations, be made to coincide with the original figure. This means that *in Euclidean geometry* lengths and angular measurements are geometric properties, because lengths and angular measurements are preserved under rotations and translations.

Projective geometry, the geometry that began with attempts by Renaissance artists to represent three-dimensional figures on two-dimensional canvases, is an example of a geometry that is defined by a different set of motions. The motions that define projective geometry are called projections. Projections preserve neither the length of a line segment nor the measure of an angle.

This may sound exotic, but it is not. Projective geometry can be used to describe how images change when they are *projected* from the film onto the movie screen. In projective geometry two different-looking triangles can be made to coincide through a series of projective "motions" even though initially the triangles may have different shapes or sizes. Therefore in projective geometry it is possible for two very different-looking triangles to be "the same." As a consequence, mathematicians who study projective geometry do not concern themselves with either lengths or angular measurements; in projective geometry lengths and angular measurements are not geometric properties.

Other geometries are defined by other sets of motions.

Mathematicians took a very long time to stretch their imagination from Euclidean geometry alone to today's wonderful diversity of geometries. They took almost as long to identify what makes a geometric property geometric: A geometric property is a property that is preserved under a group of motions. It is a surprising kind of description. Geometry can seem so static, and yet each geometry is defined by a group of motions.

In this volume we trace the history of geometry, a story of imagination and creativity and hard work. We see how some ideas and some problems have been passed from one generation of mathematicians to the next, how each generation has brought new insights and new techniques to bear on these problems, and how each generation of mathematicians has expanded on the original idea and reinterpreted what sometimes were first viewed as relatively simple problems. Simple and complex, concrete and abstract—these contrasting descriptions characterize geometry. It is a subject whose history is at least as old as civilization.

Geometry continues to change and evolve. Mathematicians' understanding of form and space continues to broaden and deepen. The great geometric problems from antiquity—problems that defied solutions for millennia by some of the finest mathematical minds in history—have now been solved, but many other, newer problems have been uncovered in the intervening years, and many of those have not yet been solved.

It is almost certainly true that some of the most interesting and important geometric problems have yet to be revealed. After more than 4,000 years of study and research, the pace of geometric discovery has never been faster. Many mathematicians feel as if they have barely scratched the surface of their subject. We can better appreciate the exciting developments of the present if we have an appreciation of the past. Developing that appreciation is the goal of this volume.

PART ONE

GEOMETRY IN ANTIQUITY

1

GEOMETRY BEFORE
THE GREEKS

Geometry begins in Egypt. That was the opinion of the fifth-century-B.C.E. Greek historian Herodotus. According to Herodotus geometry began out of necessity. Each year the Nile River overflowed its banks and washed across the fertile fields that lay in the Nile floodplain. The river would sometimes destroy boundary markers or change course and wash away plots of land. The farmers were taxed according to their landholdings, so after a flood the fields had to be resurveyed in order to establish field boundaries and tax rates. The motivation for the development of Egyptian geometry was, apparently, the desire for quick and accurate methods of surveying the farmers' fields. In response to these simple demands the Egyptians soon developed a simple geometry of mensuration, the part of geometry that consists of the techniques and concepts involved in measurement.

One of the principal tools of these early applied mathematicians was a length of rope that could be stretched into a triangle. In fact these early surveyor–mathematicians were called rope stretchers. The idea is simple enough. Suppose that a rope is divided—perhaps by knots—into 12 equal segments. When it is stretched into a triangle so that three units of rope make up one side of the triangle, four units of rope make up the second side, and five units of rope the third side, the triangle has the shape of a right triangle. The angles of the rope triangle can be used to make simple angular measurements. The rope is a convenient tool for making linear measurements as well. Simple rope techniques were, apparently,

The Great Pyramid at Giza. Egyptian monuments are usually extremely massive and geometrically simple. (Library of Congress, Prints and Photographs Division)

just what was necessary for the Egyptians to make quick and accurate surveying measurements. The skill with which they did this made a big impression on their neighbors the Greeks.

Egyptian interest in geometry did not extend much beyond what was needed for practical purposes. They developed formulas—some of which were more accurate than others—to measure certain simple areas and simple volumes. They developed, for example, a formula for computing the area enclosed within a circle. It was not an exact formula, but for practical purposes an exact formula is generally no better than a good approximation, and the Egyptians did not usually distinguish between the two. The error in their estimate of the area enclosed within a circle arose when they approximated the number π by the number 3 plus a small fraction. We also introduce some error into our calculations whenever we enter π into our calculators and for just the same reason. Unlike us, however, they were either unaware of or unconcerned by the resulting error.

In the study of three-dimensional figures, the Egyptians, not surprisingly, were interested in the geometric properties of pyramids. Given the length of the base and the height of a pyramid, for example, they could compute the volume of the pyramid. (This is important because it relates two linear measurements, height and length, to a volume. Linear measurements are often easier to make than volumetric ones.) They also described other mathematical properties of the pyramid. For example, given the length of the base of a pyramid and its height they knew how to compute a number that characterized the steepness of the sides of the pyramid. (This number is similar to—but not equal to—the slope of a line that students compute in an introductory algebra course.) In mathematics the Egyptians got off to a quick start. They worked on a wide variety of two- and three-dimensional problems early in their history. Egyptian mathematics soon stopped developing, however. For more than 2,000 years Egyptian mathematics remained largely unchanged.

For much of its long history ancient Egyptian geometry remained at a level that today's high school student would find easily accessible. This comparison can, however, be misleading. Compared to our number system, the Egyptian number system was awkward, and their methods for doing even simple arithmetic and geometry were often more complicated than ours. As a consequence although the problems they investigated may not have been harder for them to understand than for us, they were certainly harder for the Egyptians to solve than they would be for us.

Our best source of knowledge about Egyptian mathematics is the Ahmes papyrus. It is a problem text, so called because it consists of a long list of problems copied onto an approximately 18-foot (5.5-m) scroll. The copier, a scribe named Ahmes (ca. 1650 B.C.E.), was probably not the author of the text. Scholars believe that the Ahmes papyrus is a copy of a papyrus that was probably several centuries older.

To convey a feeling for the type of geometry the Egyptians found appealing we paraphrase problem 51 from the Ahmes papyrus, also called the Rhind papyrus. In problem 51 Ahmes computes the area of an isosceles triangle. (An isosceles triangle is a triangle with the property that two of its sides are of equal length.) To find the area of the triangle Ahmes imagines cutting the triangle right down the center, along the triangle's line of symmetry. Two identically shaped right triangles result. Then he imagines joining the two triangles along their hypotenuses so as to form a rectangle (see the accompanying illustration). He reasons that the area of the resulting rectangle equals the area of the original, isosceles triangle. He does so because he knows how to find the area of a rectangle. The area of the rectangle is its height times its width. The height of his rectangle equals the height of the isosceles triangle. The width of the rectangle is half of the width of the triangle. His conclusion is that the area of the triangle equals the height of the triangle times one-half the length of the triangle's base. Briefly: (Area of triangle) = 1/2 × (width of base) × (height). He is exactly right, of course.

The Egyptians were not the only people studying geometry in the time before the Greeks. Perhaps the most mathematically advanced culture of the time was that of the Mesopotamians. Mesopotamia was situated roughly 1,000 miles (1,600 km) from Egypt in what is now Iraq. Mesopotamian architecture is less well known than that of the Egyptians because the Egyptians built their monoliths of stone and the Mesopotamians built theirs of less durable mud brick. Mesopotamian mathematics, however, is now better known than Egyptian mathematics because the clay tablets that the Mesopotamians used to record their mathematics turned out to be far more durable than Egyptian papyrus. Whereas only a few original Egyptian mathematics texts survive, hundreds of Mesopotamian mathematics tablets have been recovered and translated. This is a small fraction of the hundreds of thousands of tablets that have been uncovered, but

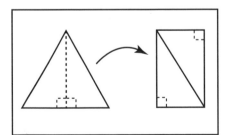

Ahmes's method for finding the area of an isosceles triangle: Cut the triangle along its line of symmetry and reassemble it in the form of a rectangle; then compute the area of the rectangle.

many nonmathematical tablets with significant math content have also been found. Astronomy tablets, for example, contain a lot of information on Mesopotamian mathematics. So do construction records, in which scribes performed fairly complicated computations to determine the amount of material required (mud bricks were the primary building material) and the number of man-hours required to complete the project.

These tablets make clear that Mesopotamian mathematicians preferred algebra to geometry, and even their geometry problems often have an algebraic feel to them. For example, the Mesopotamians knew what we call the Pythagorean theorem many centuries before Pythagoras was born. (The Pythagorean theorem states that in a right triangle the square of the length of the hypotenuse equals the sum of the squares of the two remaining sides.) Their tablets contain many problems that involve the Pythagorean theorem, but the emphasis in the problems is on solving the resulting equation, so the Pythagorean theorem simply provides another source of solvable algebraic problems.

The Mesopotamians were interested in geometry primarily as a set of techniques to assist them in their measurements and computations. Like that of the Egyptians, theirs was primarily a geometry of mensuration. They could, for example, compute the volume of an object that had the shape of a city wall—a three-dimensional form with straight sides that is thicker at the bottom than at the top but their emphasis was on the mud brick wall, not the abstract form. Their apparent motivation was to find the number of bricks that had to be made and the number of man-hours required in building the wall. They were more interested in estimating costs than in investigating geometrical forms. For the Mesopotamians, geometry was a means to an end.

The Mesopotamians had a much deeper understanding of numbers and of the techniques of computation than did the Egyptians. As a consequence they developed approximations of solutions that were far more accurate than those of their Egyptian counterparts. This is especially true in algebra, but it is also true that some of the geometric problems that they solved were more advanced than those studied in Egypt. The

Egyptians, for example, were apparently unaware of the general statement of the Pythagorean theorem. The Mesopotamians understood the Pythagorean theorem at a much deeper level and could solve a variety of problems associated with it. Some of those problems would challenge a well-educated nonmathematician today. As the Egyptians, however, the Mesopotamians did not usually distinguish between an exact solution and a good approximation. Nor, apparently, was there much interest among Mesopotamian mathematicians in proving that the results they obtained were correct. They demonstrated little interest in developing a rigorous approach to the subject of geometry as a whole.

Egyptian and Mesopotamian mathematicians were primarily concerned with developing a practical geometry. They sought to find and use mathematical formulas to compute areas and volumes of specific common geometrical forms given certain linear measurements. (Given the diameter of a circle, for example, what is the area?) The methods that the Egyptians developed for expressing their numerical answers were quite different from those developed by the Mesopotamians, however. The Egyptians counted in base 10, as we do, and they wrote their numbers using symbols specific to each power of 10. Writing the number 320, for example, involved writing (or drawing) the symbol for 100 three times and the symbol for 10 twice. Notice that this method for numeration, changing the order in which symbols are listed, does not alter the value of the number. By contrast, the Mesopotamians counted in base 60, and they wrote their numbers using an almost complete system of positional numeration that is, in concept, similar to what we use today: Rather than using 10 digits, as we do, they used 59 digits to write any number; for numbers larger than 59 they simply recycled the digits into the next column—the value of each digit depended on the column in which it appeared.

Although the methods that each culture used to express its numbers were very different, the geometrics developed by the two cultures were similar in concept because both groups of mathematicians sought numerical answers to resolve computational problems.

Theirs was a geometry of mensuration. There were no overarching ideas in their work, nor did they develop a theoretical context in which to place the formulas that they discovered. Theirs was a mathematics that was done one problem at a time; it was not mathematics in the common sense. Today, mathematicians interested in geometry are generally concerned with deducing the properties of broad classes of geometric objects from general principles. This "modern" approach is, however, not modern at all. It dates back to antiquity and to the earliest of all mathematical cultures with a modern outlook.

2

EARLY GREEK GEOMETRY

The approach of the Mesopotamians and the Egyptians to geometry was characteristic of that of all known ancient cultures with a tradition of mathematics with the exception of the Greeks. From the outset the Greek approach to mathematics was different. It was more abstract and less computational. Greek mathematicians investigated the properties of classes of geometric objects. They were concerned not only with *what* they knew, but with *how* they knew it. Nowhere is this emphasis more easily seen than in the work of the Greek philosopher and mathematician Thales of Miletus (ca. 650–ca. 546 B.C.E.).

According to Greek accounts, Thales was the first in a long line of Greek mathematicians and philosophers. He was more than a mathematician and philosopher, however. Greek accounts also describe him as a businessman, who, during a particularly good olive growing year, bought up all the olive presses in his district in order to establish a monopoly in that area during that season. (Although he could have charged exorbitant prices when the olives ripened, they say he did not. Apparently he just wanted to see whether he could corner the market.) Thales traveled widely and received his early education in geometry from the Egyptians. He must have proved an apt student because before leaving Egypt he measured the height of the Great Pyramid at Giza in a way that is so clever that his method is still remembered 2,500 years later. On a sunny day he placed a stick vertically into the ground and waited until the shadow of the stick equaled the height of the stick. At that point he measured the length of the shadow of the pyramid, because he knew that at

*Greek ruin. The Greeks were the most sophisticated geometers of antiquity.
Their temple designs reflected their sense of mathematical aesthetics.*
(Library of Congress, Prints and Photographs Division)

that instant the length of the pyramid's shadow equaled the height of the pyramid.

Thales has been credited with the discovery of many interesting facts about geometry. Perhaps the stories are true. Compared with descriptions of the accomplishments of the Egyptians, historical accounts of Thales make him look very well informed, indeed. In the late 19th century, however, as archeologists began to uncover Mesopotamian cuneiform tablets and scholars began to decode the marks that had been pressed into them, they were surprised, even shocked, to learn that more than a thousand years before Thales, the Mesopotamians had a knowledge of mathematics that far exceeded that of the Egyptians and probably of Thales as well. Perhaps Thales had traveled more widely than the stories indicate. Perhaps he had also learned from the Mesopotamians. Still it is not just what Thales knew that is important to the history of geometry; it is how he knew it. There is no better example of this distinction than the following theorem—a theorem that has been consistently attributed to Thales: A circle is bisected by a diameter.

MATH WITHOUT NUMBERS

How did the Greeks investigate the geometric properties of figures without reference to numbers or measurements? The best way to answer this question is an example. This classical proof about the measures of the angles of a triangle is a paraphrase of a proof from *Elements,* one of the most famous of all ancient Greek mathematics texts. An especially elegant proof, it is a good example of purely geometric thinking, and it is only three sentences long.

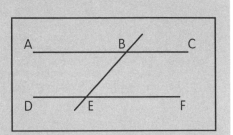

Line ABC *is parallel to line* DEF.
Line EB *is called the transversal.*
Angle ABE *equals angle* BEF

To appreciate the proof one must know the following two facts:

FACT 1: We often describe a right angle as a 90° angle, but we could describe a right angle as the angle formed by two lines that meet perpendicularly. In the first case we describe an angle in terms of its measure. In the second case we describe a right angle in terms of the way it is formed. The descriptions are equivalent, but the Greeks used only the latter. With this description the Greeks described a straight (180°) angle as the sum of two right angles.

FACT 2: When we cut two parallel lines with a third, transverse line, the interior angles on opposite sides of the transverse line are equal. (This sounds complicated, but the diagram makes clear what that complicated sentence means.) Notice that no measurement is

In this theorem the word *diameter* means a straight-line segment passing through the center of the circle and terminating on the sides. What Thales showed is that a diameter—any diameter—cuts a circle into two equal parts. This is a remarkable result—not because it is surprising but because it is obvious. Any drawing of a circle and one of its diameters makes it clear that the diameter

involved. We can be sure that corresponding angles are equal even when we do not know their measure.

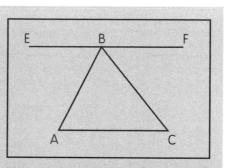

These two facts taken together are all we need to know to show that the sum of the interior angles of a triangle equals 180°, or as the Greeks would say:

The sum of the interior angles of a triangle equals the sum of two right angles.

Diagram accompanying the proof that the sum of the interior angles of a right triangle equals the sum of two right angles

(Refer to the accompanying diagram of the triangle as you read the few sentences that make up the proof.)

Proof: Call the given triangle *ABC*. Draw a line *EBF* so that line *EBF* is parallel to line *AC*.

1. Angle *CAB* equals angle *ABE*. (This is FACT 2.)

2. Angle *ACB* equals angle *CBF*. (This is FACT 2 again.)

3. The sum of the interior angles of the triangle, therefore, equals angle *ABE* plus angle *ABC* plus angle *CBF*. These angles taken together form the *straight angle EBF*. Notice again that this type of reasoning does not require a protractor; nor does it make use of any numbers or measurements. It is pure geometrical reasoning, the type of reasoning at which the Greeks excelled.

bisects the circle. Mesopotamian and Egyptian mathematicians never questioned this fact. Almost certainly Thales did not question it, either, and yet he felt the need to *deduce* the result, that is, to *prove* the truth of the statement.

This was a new way of thinking about mathematics: an approach that deemphasizes intuition and instead emphasizes the importance of deductive reasoning. Deductive reasoning, the process of reasoning from general principles to specific instances, is the characteristic that makes mathematics special. Mathematics is a deductive discipline. All mathematicians today work by beginning with known principles and then deriving new facts as logical consequences of those principles, but Thales was the first to apply this method rigorously.

Thales is also credited with other geometric results, some of which are more obvious than others. Significantly he apparently proved his results from general principles and without an appeal to intuition. In the history of geometry Thales's importance lies largely in his approach to mathematics. This approach makes Thales the first true mathematician.

We have to be careful, however, when we consider the accomplishments of Thales and his successors in ancient Greece. Though their approach to mathematics was in many ways a modern one, their understanding was, nevertheless, quite different from ours. Because of the way we learn mathematics today our first impulse is to assign a number to a quantity. For example, we have already seen that the Greeks understood the word *diameter* to mean a line segment whereas many of us identify the word *diameter* with a number—the distance across a circle. The Greeks also had a much narrower conception of number than we do. In any case their geometry developed in such a way that they often did not need to use numbers or algebraic symbolism to express their ideas. Instead they *constructed* their geometric insights. Often they used a straightedge and compass to construct a figure with certain properties. Once the figure was established all that was left was to deduce the properties of the figure from their knowledge of the techniques used in its construction and any relevant, previously established geometric facts.

This is not to say that the Greeks measured their drawings to see whether, for example, two angles were "really" equal. They did not. They were not even very careful in making their drawings. Their compasses and straightedges were often very simple, even crude, and their drawings were often made in pits of sand or in sand that was sprinkled on a flat, hard surface. The straightedge and compass drawings that they made were only aids that they used to help them imagine and communicate their ideas. When they examined three-dimensional problems they restricted their attention to relatively simple geometric forms: cylinders, spheres, cones, and the like. They obtained curves by considering the intersection of various three-dimensional forms with planes. This approach is not at all easy for modern readers to follow because we are accustomed to expressing our ideas algebraically. Algebra makes many Greek arguments easier to follow, but the Greeks themselves did not begin to develop algebra until the very end of their interest in mathematics. Consequently although the Greek *approach* to mathematics was deductive, logical, and, in many ways, very modern, the way that the Greeks *expressed* their results was different from what most of us are accustomed to today.

The Pythagoreans

The next important Greek mathematician, who, according to legend, was a student of Thales, is Pythagoras of Samos (ca. 582–ca. 500 B.C.E.). Unlike Thales, who was a man of business, Pythagoras was a mystic. He was more interested in numbers than in geometry, and his interest stemmed from religious as well as mathematical convictions. (Certain numbers were important in Pythagorean religious beliefs.) As Thales did, Pythagoras traveled widely as a young man. By the time he finally settled down he was something of a cult figure. Surrounded by followers, Pythagoras established a somewhat secretive community where property was shared and no one took individual credit for any mathematical discoveries. As a consequence we cannot know what Pythagoras discovered and what was the work of his followers. We can, however, be sure that he was not the first to discover the Pythagorean theorem. We have already seen that the theorem that bears Pythagoras's name was known and used extensively by the Mesopotamians more than a thousand years before Pythagoras's birth. Some say that he was the first to *prove* the theorem; perhaps he was, but there is no evidence to support this claim. None of this diminishes his importance in the history of mathematics, however.

Pythagoras's effect on mathematics and philosophy was profound. The most important discoveries of the Pythagoreans concerned numbers and ratios. "All is number" was the Pythagorean maxim. They believed that the universe itself could be described by using only counting numbers and ratios of counting numbers. (The expression *counting numbers* refers to the numbers belonging to the sequence 1, 2, 3, . . ., that is, the set of positive integers.) The Pythagoreans made one of the most important discoveries in the history of mathematics: what we call irrational numbers. An *irrational number* is a number that cannot be represented as a ratio of whole numbers. (The number √2, for example, is an irrational number.) This discovery proved that the Pythagorean idea that everything could be represented by whole number ratios is false, a fact that they supposedly tried to keep secret. In any case the discovery of irrational numbers showed that intuition is not always a good guide in discerning mathematical truths.

The Pythagoreans are also usually given credit for discovering what later became known as the golden section. The golden section is a specific ratio, which the Greeks represented as the ratio between two line segments. An easy way to see the golden section is to consider a star pentagon (see the accompanying figure). The distance *AC* divided by the distance *AB* is an instance of the golden section. Furthermore the distance *AD* divided by the distance *BE* is another instance of the golden section.

The golden section is sometimes described as "self-propagating." To see an example of what this means notice that the interior of the star itself is a pentagon. By connecting every other corner we can obtain another star and more examples of the

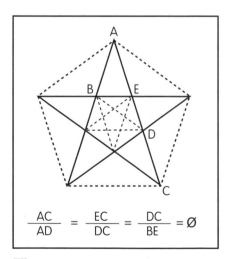

$$\frac{AC}{AD} = \frac{EC}{DC} = \frac{DC}{BE} = \varnothing$$

The star pentagon contains many examples of the golden section.

THE GOLDEN SECTION

The discoveries that the Pythagoreans (and later generations of Greek mathematicians) made about the golden section resonated throughout Greek culture. Even mathematicians of the European Renaissance, 2,000 years after the life of Pythagoras, were fascinated by the properties of the golden section. We can recapture some of the wonder with which these mathematicians regarded this ratio when we see how the golden section appears (and reappears!) in geometry, in human anatomy, and in botany.

The Greeks incorporated the golden section into their architecture because they believed it to be the rectangular form most pleasing to the eye. They designed many of their temples so that the proportions of many important lengths in the temple façade equaled the golden section. A rectangle with this property is sometimes called a golden rectangle. This rectangle has a peculiar property that demonstrates how the golden ratio is "self-propagating." If we subtract away a square with the property that one side of the square coincides with the original golden rectangle we are left with another rectangle, and this rectangle, too, is a golden rectangle. This process can continue indefinitely (see the illustration).

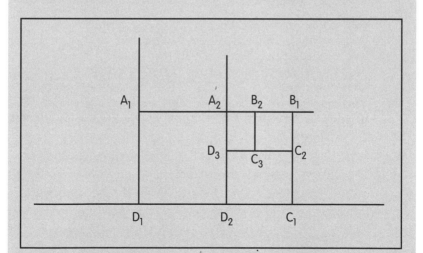

Rectangles $A_1B_1C_1D_1$, $A_2B_1C_1D_2$, $A_2B_1C_2D_3$, and $A_2B_2C_3D_3$ are golden rectangles.

(continues)

THE GOLDEN SECTION
(continued)

The golden section also appears repeatedly in the proportions used in landscape painting in Western art up until the beginning of the 20th century. These uses of the golden section are, of course, by design. What is just as remarkable is that the golden section appears frequently in nature as well.

It is sometimes convenient to represent the golden section with a number. The ratio of the lengths that determine the golden section determines a number that is often denoted with the Greek letter φ, or phi (pronounced FEE). It is an irrational number that is approximately equal to 1.618. Here are some places where φ can be found:

- In the adult human body the ratio between a healthy person's height and the vertical height of the navel very closely approximates the golden section as is the vertical height of the navel divided by the distance from the navel to the top of the head. (For adolescents, who are still in the process of growing, the ratio between total height and navel height is not a good approximation to the golden section.)

- The well-known Fibonacci series is closely related to the golden section.

- The distribution of leaves, stems, and seeds in plants is frequently organized in such a way as to yield the golden section. Leaves and stems organized about the golden section or ratio are "optimally" placed in the sense that they gather the most sunshine and cast the least shade on each other. (The mathematical proof of this fact was discovered in the late 20th century.)

- The curve called the logarithmic spiral, a form that can be found in many animal horns and spiral shells, is closely related to the golden section. (Demonstrating this would take us too far away from the history of Greek geometry, however.)

As we become more aware of the golden section, we can see how art, mathematics, and nature mirror one another in the sense that the golden section occurs frequently as an organizing principle in both natural and human-made forms. It reflects a remarkable connection between mathematics and the material world.

golden section. Similarly by extending the sides of the pentagon that surrounds our original star we obtain a new, larger star and still more examples of the golden section. This procedure can be continued indefinitely.

The golden section was an important discovery to the Pythagoreans. They used the star as their own special symbol, but they had no monopoly on the ratio. Greek architects incorporated the golden section in the proportions of the buildings that they designed. It is present in the proportions used in Greek art, and the golden section can be found throughout nature as well (see the sidebar The Golden Section). Many remarkable properties of this ratio have been uncovered during the last few millennia. Discoveries of this nature profoundly affected the Pythagoreans, who believed that numbers were the building blocks of nature.

Geometry in Athens

When we think of Greece we generally think of Athens, the capital of present-day Greece. The Parthenon is, after all, located in Athens, as are many other elegant ruins. If we think more expansively about ancient Greece we might imagine that it included all of present-day Greece. This is a much larger area than the ancient city-state of Athens but not nearly as large as Magna Graecia, the area that was once inhabited by the Greeks. Nor did the Greeks hesitate to travel beyond even Magna Graecia. Greek mathematicians were no exception. They generally moved around a lot. Pythagoras, as we have already seen, traveled widely and eventually settled in a town on the southeastern coast of what is now Italy in the Greek city of Crotona (modern Crotone). Little is known of Thales' habits except that he was fond of traveling. Archimedes, who is often described as one of the greatest mathematicians in history, was educated in Alexandria, Egypt, and lived in the Greek city-state of Syracuse. (Syracuse was located on what is now the Italian island of Sicily.) Eudoxus, who did live in Athens for a time, was from present-day Turkey and to present-day Turkey he eventually returned. Many more of the best-known Greek mathematicians lived much of their adult life in Alexandria. Few well-known mathematicians lived in what is now Greece.

Though Athens was not the home of many mathematicians, a few of them lived in Athens, which seems to be the place three of the most famous problems in Greek geometry originated. The first, which involves the problem of doubling a cube, began with a terrible plague. Around 430 B.C.E. the people of Athens were dying in great numbers. In desperation they turned to an oracle for help. The oracle they consulted, the most famous oracle in the Greek world, was located on the island of Delos. The oracle advised them to double the size of the altar in their temple to Apollo. The altar was in the shape of a cube. (To appreciate the math problem, recall that if we let the letter l represent the length of the edge of a cube then the volume of the cube is simply $l \times l \times l$ or l^3.) In their haste to follow the advice of the oracle, the Athenians constructed a new cubical altar with an edge that was twice as long as the edge of the old one. This was a mistake. The height of the new altar was twice that of the original, but so was its width and so was its depth. As a consequence, the *size*, or volume, of the new altar was $(2l) \times (2l) \times (2l)$ or $8l^3$. The new altar was *eight times the size* of the original altar instead of just twice as big. From this unhappy experience arose one of the three great classical Greek geometry problems: Given a cube, use a straightedge and compass to construct a line segment that represents the edge of a new cube whose volume is twice that of the given cube. In other words, find the dimensions of a new cube whose volume is twice that of the original by *using only a straightedge and compass.*

Also in Athens, at about the same time, two other problems were proposed. One of them was about division of an angle into three equal parts: Given an arbitrary angle, divide it into three equal parts, *using only a straightedge and compass.* The third problem has worked its way into our language. You may have heard people speak of "squaring the circle" when describing something they considered impossible to accomplish. This phrase summarizes the third classical problem: Given a circle and *using only a straightedge and compass,* construct a square with the same area as the given circle.

You can see that the common thread uniting all three problems is to find a solution by using only a straightedge and compass. This restriction is critical. The problem of doubling the cube, for example, was quickly solved by the Greek mathematician Archytas of Tarentum (ca. 428–ca. 347 B.C.E.), but his method involved manipulating three curved surfaces. His was a beautiful, though very technical, solution. It also required Archytas to work in three dimensions. Archytas's solution is not one that can be duplicated by using only a straightedge and compass, and to the Greeks it *seemed* that the doubling-the-cube problem should be solvable with the use of only these simple implements. So it was really an intellectual problem that the Greeks were determined to solve. The same is true of the other two problems.

These three problems drew the attention of mathematicians for more than 2,000 years. The problems were never solved geometrically because with only a straightedge and compass they *cannot be solved.* That is an entirely different statement from saying that the solution has not been found yet. The solution was not found because it does not exist. This remarkable fact was discovered by using a new and very powerful type of algebra developed during the 19th century.

In addition to being the birthplace of three famous mathematical problems Athens was, of course, home to many philosophers. Socrates (ca. 469–ca. 399 B.C.E.), for example, was an Athenian, but Socrates did not make many contributions to the mathematical sciences. Here is what he had to say about mathematics:

> for I cannot satisfy myself that, when one is added to one, the one to which the addition is made becomes two, or that the two units added together make two by reason of the addition.
>
> *(Plato. Phaedo. Translated by Benjamin Jowett. New York: Oxford University Press, 1892)*

Since Socrates could not convince himself that 1 plus 1 equals 2, we should not be surprised that he did not contribute much to mathematics.

Socrates' student Plato loved mathematics. He apparently had learned about mathematics from the Pythagoreans. After Pythagoras's death, the Pythagoreans at Crotona were attacked and many of them killed. The remaining disciples were scattered about Magna Graecia, and later they were no longer so secretive about the discoveries made at Crotona. Knowledge of the mathematics of the Pythagoreans made a deep impression on Plato. Plato eventually founded his own school in Athens and at his school Plato encouraged his students to study mathematics. Plato was not much of a mathematician himself, but one of his students, Eudoxus of Cnidus (ca. 408 B.C.E.–ca. 355 B.C.E.), became the foremost mathematician of his generation.

Eudoxus traveled widely for the sake of his art. Cnidus, Eudoxus's hometown, was, as noted previously, in present-day Turkey. He was originally a student of Archytas and later, briefly, became a student of Plato, who was also a friend of Archytas. (In fact, Archytas helped save Plato's life when Plato faced execution in Athens, which was always a dangerous place to practice philosophy.) Eudoxus later left Athens and founded his own school in Cyzicus, also in present-day Turkey. Eudoxus was well known as an astronomer as well as a mathematician. In geometry Eudoxus discovered what is now known as the method of exhaustion, a profound insight into mathematics that is also useful outside mathematics. Eudoxus's method allowed the Greeks to solve many problems that were previously beyond reach. The method of exhaustion is the Greek counterpart to the idea of a limit, which is the main idea underlying the subject of calculus, discovered 2,000 years later.

The idea behind the method of exhaustion is that we can represent our answer as the limit of a sequence of steps. The more steps we take, the closer we get to our answer. The method of exhaustion is not a formula for finding an exact answer. Instead it describes a general criterion that a successful formula or process must meet to ensure that our process approaches the answer that we desire. Depending on the particular process that we devise we may be close to our answer five steps into the process or we may need to repeat the process a thousand times before we are close enough. (We decide what "close enough" means.) Furthermore, it may well be that our process never yields precisely the answer we want. What is important is that the method of exhaustion guarantees that the difference between the exact answer and our approximate answer will be as small as we want *provided we repeat our process often enough*. The effect of the method of exhaustion on the subsequent development of Greek mathematics was profound.

3

MAJOR MATHEMATICAL WORKS OF GREEK GEOMETRY

Elements by Euclid of Alexandria

Euclid is one of the best-known mathematicians in history; or to be more precise, Euclid has one of the best-known names in the history of mathematics. Almost everything else about him is a mystery. We know he was working hard on mathematics around the year 300 B.C.E. in the city of Alexandria in what is now Egypt. We do not know when he was born or when he died. We do not know his birthplace. He is called Euclid of Alexandria because he worked at the museum at Alexandria, the school and library that attracted many of the best Greek mathematicians.

We know that Euclid wrote a number of books, a few of which have survived. The best known of Euclid's works is called *Elements.* It is the best-selling, most widely translated, most influential mathematics book of all time. Few—perhaps none—of the theorems and proofs in Euclid's work were discovered by Euclid, however. Some of the results in the *Elements* were almost certainly discovered by Eudoxus, but for the most part we do not know whom to credit for the different ideas we find in the book because Euclid does not tell us. Most of the results—perhaps all of the results—described in the *Elements* were probably already well known to the mathematicians of his time. Furthermore, Euclid never referred to this geometry as Euclidean. Nevertheless, the

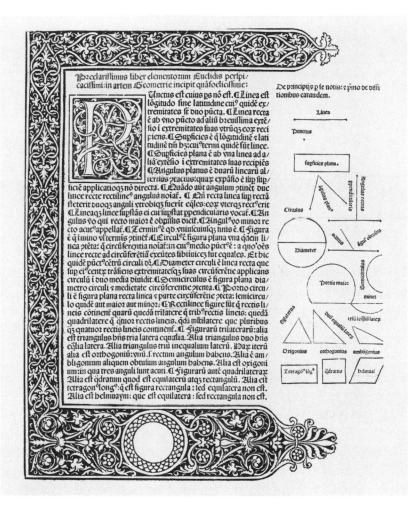

Title page of 1482 edition of Euclid's Elements (Library of Congress, Prints and Photographs Division)

type of geometry described in Euclid's book is now known as Euclidean geometry.

The *Elements* has a very broad scope because it was written more as a textbook than as a guide to mathematical research. The book is organized into 13 "books" or chapters. The first book is an introduction to the fundamentals of geometry, and the remaining 12 books survey many of the ideas that were most important to the mathematicians of the time. Of particular interest to us are the following:

- There is an extensive description of what has become known as geometric algebra, although Euclid did not call it that. (The Greeks of Euclid's day had not yet developed much algebra, but they needed to use the kinds of ideas that we would express algebraically. They responded by expressing these ideas in geometric language rather than in the algebraic symbolism with which we are familiar.)

- He covers the topic that we would identify as irrational numbers, which he called the problem of incommensurables.

- He proves that there are infinitely many prime numbers.

- He covers Eudoxus's method of exhaustion.

- He proves many theorems in plane geometry. (The preceding proof that the sum of the angles of a triangle equals the sum of two right angles is taken, more or less, from the *Elements*.)

- And he proves some theorems in solid geometry, or the geometry of three-dimensional objects.

Elements is a remarkable textbook that is still worth reading. (A few schools still use Euclid's work as a textbook, and even today most plane geometry textbooks are modeled on parts of the *Elements*.)

One reason Euclid's work is so important is that it survived when so many other texts did not, so it is our best glimpse—a very carefully written and beautiful crafted glimpse—into Greek geometric thinking. It contains many ideas and theorems that the Greeks held dear. The main importance of Euclid's work, however—the reason that it has influenced so many generations of mathematicians and scientists—lies in the way Euclid approached geometry. The *Elements* is the earliest surviving work that demonstrates what is now called the axiomatic approach to mathematics. All branches of mathematics use this approach now, but Euclid's work set the standard for almost 2,000 years.

Earlier when we said that Thales, the first Greek mathematician, *proved* new results in geometry, we did not examine exactly what that entails. Nor probably did Thales. In geometry we discover new results by deducing them from previously known ones. One result leads logically to the next. But when we prove a new geometric result, how do we know that the previous statements—the ones that we used to prove our new result—are true as well? If you spend much time with young children, you have almost certainly had the kind of conversation in which the child asks you a question and you answer it, and then the child asks, "Why?" At that point, you know there is no escape. The routine is always the same: You answer the first why question, and the child asks, "Why?" again, and again, and again. Each of your answers takes you one step further back from the original question, but because there is no final answer, you never get any closer to satisfying the child's curiosity.

It is not just children who continually ask why and remain dissatisfied with the answers they receive. Early Greek mathematicians were also faced with an endless series of unsatisfying answers. What they wanted was a logical way of exploring geometry, but what they had discovered instead was an endless chain of logical implications. They could prove that condition C was a logical consequence of condition B; they could prove that condition B was a logical consequence of condition A; but why was condition A true? For children the situation is hopeless. It may sound equally hopeless for mathematicians, but it is not. Euclid knew the answer.

Euclid begins the very first section of the first book of the *Elements* with a long list of definitions—a sort of mathematical glossary—and then follows this list with a short list of axioms and postulates. Euclid places the axioms and postulates at the beginning of his work because they are so important to the subject he loves. The axioms and postulates are the basic building blocks of his geometry. (Euclid made a distinction between the axioms, which he believed were fairly obvious and universally applicable, and the postulates, which were narrower in scope. Both the axioms and the postulates served the same function, however, and today mathematicians make no distinction between axioms and postulates.) Euclid listed five axioms and five postulates. He asserted that these 10 properties constituted an exhaustive list of the fundamental characteristics of the geometry that we now call Euclidean geometry. The axioms and postulates are *assumed* true. They do not require proof. In fact, they *cannot* be proved either true or false within this geometry *because the axioms and postulates determine what the geometry is.* Axioms and postulates are like the rules of the game. If we change them, we change the geometry itself. They are the ultimate answer to the question, Why is this true? Any true statement in Euclidean geometry is true because in the end it is a consequence of one or more of Euclid's axioms and postulates.

Euclid's goal was an ambitious one. Any set of axioms and postulates must meet certain criteria. First, the axioms cannot contradict one another; otherwise, we eventually uncover a statement that can be proved both true *and* false. (Preventing this is important.) Second, the axioms and postulates need to be logically independent; that means that no axiom or postulate can be a logical consequence of the others. (We do not want to derive one axiom as a consequence of another one.) Finally, any set of axioms or postulates has to be complete: That is, all theorems should be logical consequences of our axioms and postulates. Finding a set of axioms that satisfies these conditions is trickier than it sounds.

A very formal, very logical approach to geometry was what made Greek geometry different from everything that went before. The Greeks introduced a new idea of what mathematical truth means. For Euclid (and for all succeeding generations of geometers) the test of whether something is true is not whether the result agrees with our senses, but rather whether the statement is a logical consequence of the axioms and postulates that describe the system. In this approach to mathematics, once a complete and consistent set of axioms is established, the act of geometric discovery consists solely of deducing previously unknown logical *consequences* from the axioms, the postulates, and any previously discovered results. In other words Euclid's goal was to make geometry a purely deductive science.

For the most part the axioms and postulates are stated in a straightforward and easy-to-understand way, and later generations of mathematicians were satisfied with most of the axioms and postulates that Euclid had chosen. An example of one of Euclid's axioms is "The whole is greater than the part." An example of one of his postulates is "A straight line can be drawn from any point to any point." Of the 10 axioms and postulates nine of them are brief and matter-of-fact. The fifth postulate is the exception. In the fifth postulate Euclid explains the conditions under which nonparallel lines meet. Also called the parallel postulate, it inspired more than 2,000 years of controversy.

The controversy was due, in part, to the complicated nature of the fifth postulate. Here is what the fifth postulate says:

> If a transversal (line) falls on two lines in such a way that the interior angles on one side of the transversal are less than two right angles, then the lines meet on that side on which the angles are less than two right angles.
>
> (*Euclid.* Elements. *Translated by Sir Thomas L. Heath.* Great Books of the Western World. *Vol. 11. Chicago: Encyclopaedia Britannica, 1952.*)

See the accompanying diagram for an illustration of the type of situation that the postulate describes. Compared with the other axioms and postulates the fifth postulate strikes many people as strangely convoluted. Almost from the start, many mathematicians suspected that one should be able to *deduce* the fifth postulate as a consequence of the other four postulates and five axioms. If that were the case—if those mathematicians were right—the fifth postulate would not be a postulate at all. Instead the fifth postulate would be a *consequence* of the other nine axioms and postulates. In that case, logically speaking, it would be a sort of fifth wheel; the fifth postulate would not be one of the fundamental properties of the geometry.

For centuries mathematicians researched the relationship between the fifth postulate and Euclid's other axioms and postulates. Many mathematicians produced "proofs" that the parallel postulate was a consequence of the other axioms and postulates,

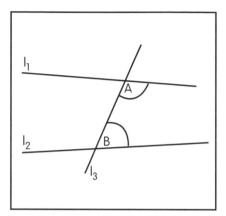

The fifth postulate states that if the sum of the measures of angles A and B is less than 180°, then lines l₁ and l₂ intersect on the same side of l₃ as A and B.

but on closer inspection each proof contained some flaw. The fifth postulate was like a pebble in the shoe of mathematicians everywhere — a continual source of irritation. For 20 centuries, however, it was Euclid's formulation of geometry that dominated mathematical thought.

Euclid attempted to axiomatize geometry—that is, he tried to establish a logically consistent and complete set of "rules" from which the entire subject of Euclidean geometry could be deduced. He almost got it right, and he was right about the fifth postulate. His parallel postulate is not a logical consequence of the other axioms and postulates. Euclid's 10 axioms and postulates are, however, not quite complete. There are several places in his work where Euclid assumes that some property or another is true even though that property cannot be deduced from the geometry as he conceived it. These mistakes are not big mistakes and they were not especially "obvious" ones, either. In fact, it was not until late in the 19th century, after mathematicians had discovered other geometries and developed a far more critical eye for such matters than the ancient Greeks ever did, that Euclid's mistakes were finally identified and corrected.

Despite these oversights, what Euclid and the other mathematicians of Magna Graecia did was a tremendous accomplishment. Only geometry reached this level of rigor until relatively recent historical times. Various disciplines in algebra, for example, were not axiomatized until the late 19th and early 20th centuries, and probability theory was not axiomatized until well into the 20th century. When a mathematical discipline can be expressed as a set of definitions and axioms and a collection of theorems derived from the axioms and definitions, mathematical truth becomes strictly testable. This was Euclid's greatest insight.

EUCLID REEXAMINED

By the end of the 19th century mathematicians had developed a number of geometries in addition to the one described by Euclid. Some of these geometries are counterintuitive; that is another way of saying that although these geometries violated no mathematical laws, our common-sense notions of space and form are of little help in understanding them. Algebra, too, became highly abstract during the 19th century. It was during that time that many mathematicians began to recognize the importance of axiomatizing all of mathematics. Their goal was to ensure that all mathematical questions would have strictly mathematical (as opposed to commonsense) answers.

One of the foremost proponents of this approach was the German mathematician David Hilbert (1862–1943). Late in the 19th century Hilbert turned his considerable intellect to Euclid's work. He identified a number of logical shortcomings in the *Elements,* most of which would never have occurred to Euclid because mathematics and logic were simply not advanced enough in Alexandria in 300 B.C.E. to make the shortcomings apparent. Hilbert rewrote Euclid's definitions and proposed replacing Euclid's five axioms and five postulates with a list of 21 axioms. These new axioms would make Euclid's geometry logically consistent and complete. Included in his list was an analog to Euclid's parallel postulate, but some of the other axioms addressed problems that would probably have struck Euclid as a little strange. For example, among his 21 axioms, Hilbert includes five that relate to order, such as "Of any three points situated on a straight line, there is always one and only one which lies between the other two" (Hilbert, David. *Foundations of Geometry.* Translated by E. J. Townsend. Chicago: Open Court Publishing Company, 1902). Seem obvious? Here is another order-related axiom: "If A, B, C are points of a straight line and B lies between A and C, then B also lies between C and A" (ibid.). The inclusion of these and similar axioms shows that what might seem obvious to us is not logically necessary. In fact, without these axioms Hilbert's formulation of Euclidean geometry would have been logically incomplete. It took well over 2,000 years, until 1899 and the publication of *The Foundations of Geometry* by David Hilbert, for Euclidean geometry finally to be made logically consistent.

The Method, On The Sphere and Cylinder, and Other Works by Archimedes

Euclid's *Elements* had an important influence on Greek mathematics and it continued to affect the direction and emphasis of mathematical thinking for millennia. The same cannot be said of the works of Archimedes of Syracuse (ca. 287 B.C.E.–ca. 212 B.C.E.). Although some of Archimedes' results became widely known and used in Greek, Islamic, and European culture, much of his work was, apparently, just too technically difficult to attract much attention. Today the situation is different. Many of the problems that Archimedes solved are now routinely solved in calculus classes. What made these problems so difficult for so long is that Archimedes solved them without the carefully developed notation, the techniques, and even some of the ideas that now characterize calculus. When we read Archimedes' works we see the results of extraordinary mathematical insight and tremendous effort. Archimedes' mathematical investigations are among the most advanced and singular works of antiquity.

A great deal has been written about Archimedes' personal life and accomplishments. We know that he was born in the Greek city-state of Syracuse, which was located on what is now the Italian island of Sicily. He was apparently educated in Alexandria, perhaps taking instruction from students of Euclid. He later returned to his home in Syracuse, where he lived for the rest of his life. He communicated his mathematical discoveries to prominent mathematicians in Alexandria, including Eratosthenes of Cyrene, who is best remembered for computing the circumference of Earth.

Most accounts of Archimedes describe a man utterly preoccupied with mathematics and science. It is an oft-told story that Archimedes did not spend much time bathing. He preferred to spend all of his time studying mathematics. When his friends forced him to take a bath, he spent his time drawing diagrams with his finger and concentrating on the ideas represented therein. More impressive to his fellow Syracusians was Archimedes' genius for designing weapons of war. Archimedes' knowledge of

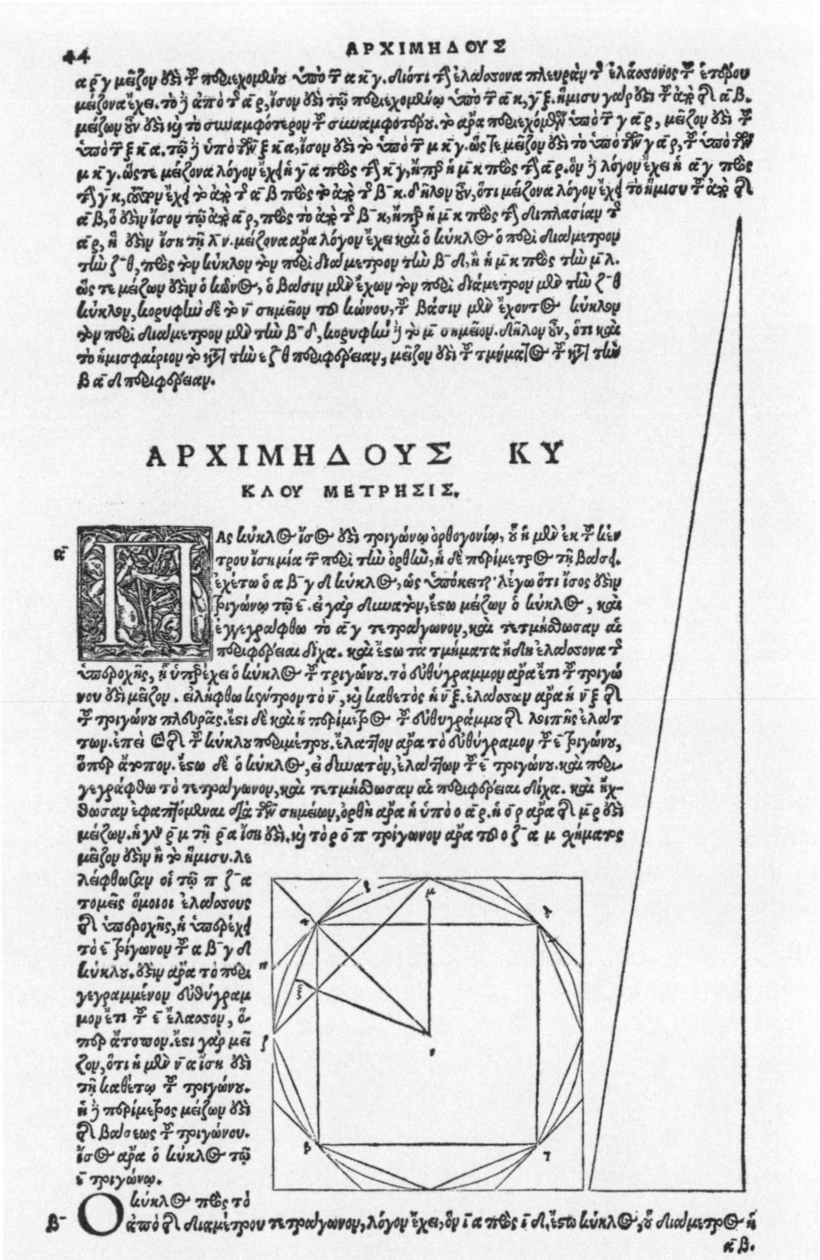
44 ΑΡΧΙΜΗΔΟΥΣ

ΑΡΧΙΜΗΔΟΥΣ ΚΥΚΛΟΥ ΜΕΤΡΗΣΙΣ.

Page of an essay by Archimedes, written in Greek and published in 1544
(Library of Congress, Prints and Photographs Division)

physics and his skill in designing simple machines enabled him to invent weapons of war that the people of Syracuse used against the attacking Roman armies. (Archimedes was already an old man when his city was under Roman attack.) His weapons prevented the Romans from conquering Syracuse by military might. In response the Romans besieged Syracuse for two years. Eventually they found a way to conquer Syracuse by subterfuge. Archimedes was killed during the sacking of the city.

Part of the plunder that the Romans took from Syracuse was a mechanical device designed by Archimedes to demonstrate a Sun-centered model of the solar system, a model that had been proposed by the Greek astronomer Aristarchus of Samos. Archimedes' device even demonstrated how eclipses occur. Although Archimedes' principal interest was geometry, he apparently enjoyed designing and building objects to demonstrate scientific ideas and principles.

Archimedes' mathematical works were almost lost to us. The Greek originals are known largely through a single text that survived into the 16th century, and one of Archimedes' works, *The Method* which is now one of his most famous works, was not rediscovered until much later. *The Method* became available to modern scholars for the first time in 1906 when it, together with some known works of Archimedes, was found in a library in Constantinople (now Istanbul, Turkey). It had remained there, unnoticed, for almost a thousand years. The book was not in good condition. Someone in the 10th century had attempted to erase the entire text and copy religious writings into the book in place of the mathematics. Fortunately the erasures were not quite complete, and most of Archimedes' work was recovered.

Of all Archimedes' mathematical discoveries, his favorite result was obtained in the two-volume work *On the Sphere and Cylinder*. In these texts Archimedes proved that the volume of a sphere is two-thirds the volume of the smallest circular cylinder that can contain it (see the accompanying diagram). This was important because the volume of the cylinder was already known: It is the area of the base multiplied by the height of the cylinder.

Archimedes was so proud of this discovery that he wanted the diagram that represented the discovery engraved on his tombstone. We know that this was done, because more than a century later the Roman writer and statesman Marcus Tullius Cicero visited Syracuse and found Archimedes' grave neglected and overgrown with weeds. He restored it.

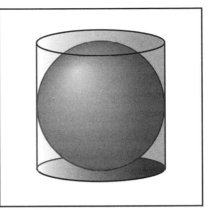

Archimedes proved that the volume of the sphere is two-thirds the size of the smallest cylinder that can contain it.

In addition to his work on three-dimensional forms, Archimedes studied curves. He wrote an entire treatise entitled *On Spirals*. Here is how he described the spiral:

> If a straight line drawn in a plane revolve at a uniform rate about one extremity which remains fixed and return to the position from which it started, and if, at the same time as the line revolves, a point move at a uniform rate along the straight line beginning from the extremity which remains fixed, the point will describe a spiral in the plane.

> (*Archimedes*. On Spirals. *Translated by Sir Thomas L. Heath*. Great Books of the Western World. *Vol. 11. Chicago: Encyclopaedia Britannica, 1952.*)

There are several important points to notice about Archimedes' choice of subject and his description of it. First, Archimedes was aware of only a small number of curves. This is true of all the Greeks. Although devoting an entire book to the study of spirals may strike some as excessive, it should be borne in mind that Archimedes had only a dozen or so curves from which to choose. This one book treats a significant fraction of all the curves of which the Greeks were aware. Second, notice that

Archimedes' description of the curve is mechanical. He is describing a physical procedure that would allow the user to trace out a spiral. There are no symbols in his work. There are no equations. This stands in stark contrast to today's approach, in which curves are generally defined by equations. Archimedes' method is very laborious.

The awkward nature of Archimedes' description arises because he uses no algebra. The Greeks had little interest in algebra. Our facility in generating new curves is due largely to our facility with algebra. For the Greeks describing almost any curve was a struggle. The length of his definition shows that even for Archimedes, one of the best mathematicians in history, describing a simple spiral meant a long, not-especially-easy-to-follow description.

In *On Spirals* Archimedes made several discoveries about the nature of this one type of spiral. For example, after one complete revolution the area bounded by the spiral and the line covers one-third the area of a circle with radius equal to the distance from the "extremity" to the position of the point on the line after one complete revolution. He goes on to prove a number of similar results. He also is able to use his spiral to solve the classical problem of trisecting an arbitrary angle, but because his solution cannot be completed by using only a straightedge and compass, he is not successful in solving the problem as posed.

Archimedes was also interested in computing various areas, a problem of great importance in mathematics and physics. In *Quadrature of the Parabola* he finds an area bounded by a parabola and a line. To do this he makes use of the method of exhaustion, an idea that foreshadowed calculus. Although Eudoxus invented the method of exhaustion, Archimedes was the most skilled mathematician in antiquity in using the concept to obtain new results. He uses it repeatedly in many of his works.

Archimedes was a prolific and creative mathematician, but many people, even mathematicians, have found reading his mathematical writings frustrating. The main problem is that Archimedes' writings on geometry are very terse. He provides the reader with little in the way of supporting work, so we often cannot know how

Archimedes performed his calculations nor how he got his ideas. That is why *The Method* is very interesting to so many people. Archimedes used *The Method* to communicate the way he begins investigating a problem. *The Method* is not mathematics in the usual sense. It is not a collection of theorems and proofs. It is Archimedes' own explanation of how he investigated an idea before he tried to prove it mathematically. This is where we can see how Archimedes' interests in mechanics and geometry meshed.

Archimedes imagined that geometrical shapes have mass, and he imagined balancing them. By determining the balance point he could compare the area or volume of a figure that he already understood with the one that he was trying to investigate. These were "thought experiments." They cannot be used in place of rigorous mathematical analyses, but they do give us insight into the way Archimedes learned. *The Method* is also an attempt by the author to stimulate mathematical research among his contemporaries and successors. Here is how he explained his reasons for writing *The Method*:

> I deem it necessary to expound the method partly because I have already spoken of it and do not want to be thought to have uttered vain words, but equally because I am persuaded that it will be of no little service to mathematics; for I apprehend that some, either of my contemporaries or of my successors, will, by means of the method when once established, be able to discover other theorems in addition, which have not yet occurred to me.
>
> (*Archimedes.* The Method. *Translated by Sir Thomas L. Heath.* Great Books of the Western World. *Vol. 11. Chicago Encyclopaedia Britannica, 1952*)

Unfortunately by the time *The Method* was rediscovered early in the 20th century, mathematics had moved on, and Archimedes' hope remained largely unfulfilled.

Conics by Apollonius of Perga

Little is known of the life of Apollonius of Perga (ca. 262 B.C.E.– ca. 190 B.C.E.). Apollonius was born in Perga, which was located in

APOLLONII PERGÆI
CONICORUM
LIBRI OCTO,

ET

SERENI ANTISSENSIS
DE SECTIONE
CYLINDRI & CONI
LIBRI DUO.

OXONIÆ,
E THEATRO SHELDONIANO, An. Dom. MDCCX.

Title page of Apollonius's Conicorum (Conics), *published in 1704* (Library of Congress, Prints and Photographs Division)

what is now Turkey. He was educated in Alexandria, Egypt, probably by students of Euclid. He may have taught at the university at Alexandria as a young man. Eventually he moved to Pergamum, which was located at the site of the present-day city of Bergama, Turkey. Pergamum was one of the most prosperous and cultured cities of its time. It had a university and a library that rivaled those at Alexandria, and it was there that Apollonius taught. Apparently he made Pergamum his permanent home. Pergamum was a prosperous and carefully planned city, built on a hill overlooking a broad, flat plain. In addition to an excellent library and university, it had a large theater built into the side of the hill. It must have been beautiful.

"The Great Geometer" was what his contemporaries called Apollonius. Today he is still known as *a* great geometer, although almost all of his mathematical writings have been lost over the intervening centuries. We know the titles of many of his works and a little about their subject matter because many of the lost works were described by other authors of the time. Two works by Apollonius were preserved for the modern reader: *Conics* and *Cutting-off of a Ratio*. *Conics* is a major mathematical work. It was written in eight volumes, of which the first seven volumes were preserved. It is here that we can see just how good a mathematician Apollonius was.

Apollonius begins *Conics* by summarizing the work of his predecessors, including Euclid. He then forges ahead to describe creative approaches to difficult problems. His analysis is careful and thorough. He sometimes provides more than one solution to the same problem because each solution offers a different insight into the nature of the problem. The discoveries Apollonius describes in his treatise resonated in the imaginations and research of mathematicians for many centuries.

So what is a conic, or, more properly, a *conic surface?* Here is how Apollonius described it:

> If from a point a straight line is joined to the circumference of a
> circle which is not in the same plane with the point, and the line
> is produced in both directions, and if, with the point remaining

fixed, the straight line being rotated about the circumference of the circle returns to the same place from which it began, then the generated surface composed of the two surfaces lying vertically opposite one another, each of which increases indefinitely as the generating straight line is produced indefinitely, I call a conic surface.

(Apollonius. Conics. Encyclopaedia Britannica, *1st ed., s.v. "Great Books of the Western World")*

Notice that Apollonius's description of conic surfaces is a rhetorical one: That is, he expresses his ideas in complete prose sentences. He uses no algebraic symbolism at all. The algebraic symbolism necessary to describe conics simply and easily would not be created for almost 2,000 more years. Because Apollonius's description is rhetorical, it is not especially easy for a modern reader to follow.

To appreciate the type of surface Apollonius described, we begin by describing a special type of conic surface, called a right conic surface, in a more modern way: Imagine a point placed directly under the center of a circle. Imagine a line passing through the point and resting on the circle. In the description that follows the point remains fixed. The line pivots about the point. To construct the conic, move the line so that it remains in contact with the circle. As it moves along the circle's circumference, it traces out a shape in space that resembles two very tall ice cream cones joined at their pointy bases. This is the conic. The point at which the two cones are joined is called the vertex of the conic. The figure is symmetric about the line that contains the pivot point and the center of the circle. This line is called the axis of symmetry of the conic (see the illustration).

From his conic surface Apollonius obtains three important curves: an ellipse, a hyperbola, and a parabola. Discovering the properties of these curves—each such curve is called a conic section—is actually much of the reason that he wrote the book. He describes each curve as the intersection of a plane with the conic surface. Alternatively we can imagine the plane as a method of cutting straight across the conic. In this case the curve is the cut we make into the conic. We begin by cutting the conic with a plane so that the plane is perpendicular to the axis of symmetry of the conic. The result is a circle. If, however, we tilt our plane slightly when we cut the conic we obtain an ellipse. The more we tilt our plane, the more elongated our ellipse is. If we continue to tilt our plane until it is parallel to a line generating the conic, it should not pass through the vertex, then we have made an infinitely long curve along either the upper or the lower cone but

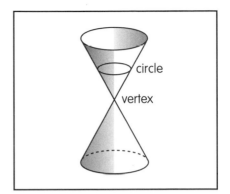

Apollonius's method of generating a cone results in the construction of two cones joined at the vertex and with the same axis of symmetry.

not both. The resulting curve is called a parabola. Finally, if we tilt our plane even more so that it cuts both the upper and lower cones—while avoiding the vertex—we see the curve called a hyperbola. The names of these curves are also due to Apollonius.

One reason that Apollonius's mathematical discoveries were important is that he learned so much about these three fundamental curves. Because the Greeks were aware of only about a dozen curves, Apollonius manages to study about a quarter of all the curves known at the time. Furthermore Apollonius's analysis was very penetrating. His work on conic sections was as advanced as any work on the subject for many centuries. In retrospect another reason that Apollonius's analyses of conic sections turned out to be so important

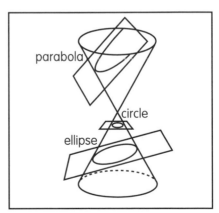

Conic sections can be represented as the intersection of a double cone and a plane.

INVESTIGATING CONIC SECTIONS

In his multivolume set *Conics,* Apollonius studied three curves: hyperbolas, parabolas, and ellipses. These are some of the simplest known curves, and yet Apollonius wrote eight volumes about their properties. How is this possible?

One reason that *Conics* is so long is that Apollonius's treatment of the subject is synthetic: That is, he uses no algebra. The diagrams that accompany the text help make his ideas clear, but without algebra the exposition is, by modern standards, very long-winded. It is not uncommon for Apollonius to take a page or two proving even a fairly simple proposition. (Of course these propositions are only simple by contemporary standards. After mathematicians learned to apply algebra to the solution of geometry problems, questions that had once challenged expert mathematicians could be assigned as homework to high school students.)

Another reason for the great length of *Conics* is that Apollonius's analysis of the subject is exhaustive. He carefully considers an extraordinary number of properties. Many of his theorems and most of his proofs are too technical to include here, but to convey a feeling for the tone of Apollonius's great work, we include Proposition 28, its diagram, and a modern explanation (not a proof) of what Apollonius is trying to prove.

Proposition 28 (book II)

If in a section of a cone or circumference of a circle some straight line bisects two parallel straight lines, then it will be a diameter of the section.

(ibid.)

The meaning of the word *diameter* when applied to a circle is well known. When Apollonius uses the word *diameter* in connection with a conic section he means an axis of symmetry of the section.

In the diagram the lines *BFA* and *DEC* are the parallel lines to which Apollonius refers in his theorem. The conic section and the two parallel lines are assumed to be given in the sense that the mathematician has no control over the choice of conic section or the placement of the parallel lines. There is one more line over which the mathematician can exercise no control: That is the line passing through the points *E* and *F.* Line *EF* bisects both lines, *BFA* and *DEC.* Apollonius's goal is to prove that in this situation line *EF* is a diameter of the conic.

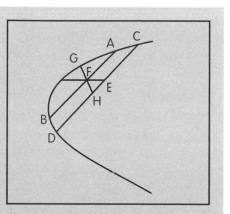

Illustration for Apollonius's theorem 28, book II

Conics is filled with theorems of this type, and if the reader is in doubt as to what the point of all this effort is, Apollonius tells us: He believes that an insightful mathematical argument is a thing of beauty. Mathematics, he says, is to be studied for its own sake.

is that conic sections have been extremely important in both science and mathematics over the succeeding centuries. For example, during the European Renaissance, Johannes Kepler correctly claimed that planets move about the Sun in elliptical orbits, and within a generation of Kepler's discovery, Isaac Newton had constructed a reflecting telescope with a parabolic, or parabola-shaped, mirror. Of course, neither of these applications was known to Apollonius. He was investigating conic sections for purely geometric reasons. He believed that imaginative, rational thought is as interesting and as beautiful as art or music.

Collection by Pappus of Alexandria

Pappus of Alexandria was the last of the great Greek geometers whose writings remain intact. The dates of his birth and death are uncertain, but we know that he lived during the third century C.E. There were almost certainly other important mathematicians in Alexandria during this time. We can be sure that Pappus was not alone because his writings contain references to other mathematicians and other lost mathematical treatises. Of some of these mathematicians and their work we now know nothing except what Pappus wrote. As a consequence it is difficult to place Pappus's work in a historical context. Most of the history is missing. That is one reason that his principal work, *Collection*, is important. Pappus's *Collection* is the last of the extant great Greek mathematical treatises.

The *Collection* consisted of eight volumes. The first volume and part of the second have been lost. In the remaining six and a half volumes Pappus describes many of the most important works in Greek mathematics. He writes about, among others, Euclid's *Elements*, Archimedes' *On Spirals*, Apollonius's *Conics*, and the works of the Greek astronomer Ptolemy. Pappus's approach is thorough. He generally introduces each important work and then describes its contents. He clearly expects the reader to read the original along with his commentary, but Pappus is not satisfied with simply reviewing the work of others. Whenever he feels it necessary or desirable, he provides alternative proofs for some of the theorems that he is reviewing. Nor is he shy about improving on the original. On occasion he contributes new ideas that are, apparently, uniquely his. For Pappus the original text is the place to begin, not end.

It is through Pappus's book, for example, that we learn of a lost work of Archimedes. In this lost work, Archimedes studied the properties of what are now called semiregular solids. Semiregular solids are three-dimensional, highly symmetric geometric forms. Pappus seems to have learned of these objects through the works of Archimedes; they are known to us through the work of Pappus. Writing reviews and commentaries on the works of others had become a common practice late in the history of Greek geometry.

But Pappus did not limit his efforts to the writing of commentaries. He was an imaginative mathematician in his own right. As many of the Greek mathematicians who preceded him were, he was interested in the solution of the three classical unsolved problems: the doubling of a cube, the trisection of an angle, and the squaring of the circle. In each case Pappus describes a solution of sorts. He describes, for example, a method for trisecting an angle that uses a hyperbola. Because this algorithm cannot be accomplished by using *only* a straightedge and compass, it is not a solution to the original problem, which states that the reader must restrict himself or herself to these implements. Nevertheless Pappus can, when *not* restricted to a straightedge and compass,

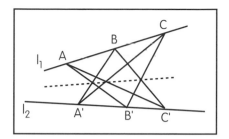

Diagram illustrating the theorem of Pappus

solve each of the three problems. In fact, he knows and describes multiple solutions for the problems, although, again, none of his solutions for any of the three problems can be derived with a straightedge and compass alone.

More importantly from a theoretical point of view, Pappus classifies geometry problems into three distinct groups. *Plane* problems, he writes, are problems that *can* be solved by using only a straightedge and compass. *Solid* problems, such as the problem of trisecting an angle, are solvable through the use of conics. Finally, he defines *linear* problems as problems that are neither plane nor solid. What is significant about this definition is that Pappus states, without proof, that the three classical unsolved problems of Greek geometry *are not plane problems!* In other words they are unsolvable as originally posed. His intuition is correct, but he does not provide a proof of this assertion.

Another discovery by Pappus is now known as the theorem of Pappus. This theorem has fascinated mathematicians for millennia because it fits nicely into more than one branch of geometry. The idea is simple enough. Suppose we imagine two lines and on each line we choose three points. We may, for example, denote the points on our first line, which we call l_1, with the letters A, B, and C and the points on our second line, l_2, with the letters A', B,' and C' (see the accompanying diagram). Now draw a line through each of the following pairs of points: (A, C'), (C, A'), (A, B'), (B, A'), (B, C'), and (C, B'). The first thing to notice is that no matter how we draw l_1 or l_2 and no matter how we choose A,

B, *C*, and *A'*, *B'*, *C'*, the points of intersection of the corresponding lines that we have just drawn always lie on a single line.
Another way of saying the same thing is that the points of intersection are collinear. Not so obvious is the curious relationship
between the nine points and nine lines of this problem. The nine
lines are grouped into sets of three lines because the three lines
intersect on a single point. Similarly the nine points are grouped
into sets of three points apiece because each set of three points
lies on a single line. This striking symmetry between the properties of the points and the properties of the lines is an example
of *duality*. Notice that if we interchange the words *line* with *point*
and *intersect* with *lies* (or vice versa) in each of the two sentences
we still get a true statement: "Each point lies on three lines" and
"Each line contains three points." Duality proved to be an
important concept in the development of projective geometry
about 15 centuries after Pappus's death, but Pappus's work contains one of the first examples of this important and surprising
property.

Pappus made several other observations that presaged important
discoveries in mathematics by many centuries. We have remarked
more than once in this chapter that the Greeks worked with a very
small vocabulary of curves. They were aware of circles, conics, spirals, and a few other curves, but until Pappus they had no
way of generating a large number of different types of
curves. Pappus actually found a way to generate many different kinds of curves, but he seems to have not recognized
the significance of his discov-ery. He begins with a problem
first solved by Apollonius for generating a conic and generalizes Apollonius's method to an algorithm for generating what have since become

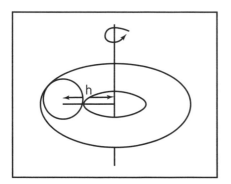

A torus can be obtained by rotating a circle about a line. Pappus found a way to calculate the volume of this type of object.

known as higher plane curves. Pappus's discovery in this area drew little attention among mathematicians for 1,300 years.

Finally, we point out that Pappus was also a master of the method of exhaustion, first described by Eudoxus 700 years earlier. Pappus used his skill with the method of exhaustion to study solids of revolution. (Mathematically a solid of revolution is obtained by rotating a two-dimensional curve about a line to obtain a three-dimensional solid. A physical expression of this idea is a table leg, baseball bat, or other object that is cut by using a lathe. The cutting tool traces out the curve as the lathe rotates the wood.) To appreciate Pappus's theorem we present a simple example: Consider a circle. If we rotate a circle about a line outside the circle we get a figure that looks a lot like a bagel. The technical term for a solid obtained in this way is a torus (see the accompanying illustration). Pappus discovered that the volume of the torus equals the area, A, enclosed by the circle times the distance that the center of A must travel about the axis of rotation. If we let h represent the distance traveled by the center of the circle, the equation that expresses the volume of the torus is $V = A \times h$.

Pappus went on to find a general formula for computing solids of revolution. Calculating the volume of a solid of revolution is the type of problem that is now usually solved over and over again in an introductory calculus class. In Pappus's time, however, the problem was much harder because (1) the concept had not been explored before, and (2) calculus had not been invented yet, and (3) using the method of exhaustion is generally more difficult than using standard calculus techniques.

The Greek mathematical tradition lasted many centuries and produced a great deal of insightful mathematics about the properties of triangles, conic sections, spirals, and the like, but what did this mathematics *mean?* When we reviewed the works of Euclid, Archimedes, Apollonius, Pappus, and others, we chose those ideas that seem to matter most today. Other results were omitted. Sometimes those mathematical results that are most important to us were not considered as important by the mathematicians responsible for their discovery. Conversely what was important to them may not seem significant to us.

THE END OF THE
GREEK MATHEMATICAL TRADITION

Pappus of Alexandria lived about 800 years after Thales of Miletus, the first of the major Greek mathematicians. Pappus's most important work, *Collection,* is the last major Greek mathematics text to survive until modern times, but it is doubtful that Pappus was the last important Greek mathematician. The museum at Alexandria remained an important place of learning and scholarship for about a century after Pappus's death.

Many historians associate the end of Greek mathematical scholarship with the death of Hypatia (ca. 370–415), a prominent mathematician and astronomer at the university at Alexandria. Hypatia wrote a number of mathematical commentaries on the works of prominent mathematicians and astronomers: *Conics* by Apollonius of Perga, *Arithmetica* by Diophantus of Alexandria, and others. Her astronomical writings included a commentary on the works of the most influential astronomer of antiquity, Ptolemy. The practice of writing commentaries on the works of other mathematicians and astronomers had become commonplace during the last centuries of the Greek mathematical tradition.

Our knowledge of Hypatia is all secondhand since none of her work survived. We know of her through some letters addressed to her by a student as well as several descriptions of her and her work by writers of the time. Hypatia was apparently a well-known public figure in Alexandria 16 centuries ago. Her prominence in mathematics and science made her a controversial figure in the disputes that were occurring between the early Christians and the pagans in Alexandria. The early Christians of Alexandria associated mathematics and science with pagan practices. The disputes between the Christians and pagans were sometimes violent. Hypatia was eventually murdered by a Christian mob, but her death did not end her influence. It had a profound impact on the scholars in Alexandria and on the subsequent development of mathematics. In reaction to her murder, many of the scholars in Alexandria decided to leave. After about 700 years as one of the foremost centers of mathematical learning in the world, Alexandria entered into a period of decline from which it has yet to recover.

Today many mathematicians are fond of pointing out that abstruse results that may seem pointless now may later prove to be very important. But as any mathematician knows, the phrase "may later prove to be important" is logically the equivalent of the phrase "may later prove to be unimportant." We should make the effort to appreciate the accomplishments of the mathematicians discussed in this chapter on their own terms. They undertook creative investigations into a world of *mathematical* ideas. Theirs was the first serious attempt to develop a deductive science. Greek mathematicians generally undertook their investigations without reference to nonmathematical criteria, and it is apparent from the work they left that that is how they wanted their work judged. They believed that their work was as aesthetically important as that of painters, musicians, and sculptors.

There is another aspect of their work, however, that they could not possibly have appreciated. Greek mathematics is also important *to us* because of the way their results were used by succeeding generations of non-Greek mathematicians. Islamic mathematicians, who were primarily interested in algebra, were also familiar with the geometry of the Greeks. Greek standards of rigor as well as Greek geometric insights influenced the development of Islamic algebra, and Islamic algebra—especially the algebra of Mohammed ibn-Mūsā al-Khwārizmī (ca. 780–ca. 850)—heavily influenced the development of algebra in Renaissance Europe. Greek mathematics also influenced the development of European science. Renaissance scientists used Greek geometry to gain insight into planetary orbits and the flight of projectiles. Isaac Newton's (1643–1727) great work *Philosophiae Naturalis Principia Mathematica* is infused with Greek ideas about mathematics, and Greek mathematics continued to be used long after Newton. As previously mentioned, David Hilbert revisited Greek geometry in 1899 when he published a revised and corrected set of axioms for Euclidean geometry. These new axioms reflected more modern ideas of rigor and a higher standard of logic, but it was the geometry of Euclid that still formed the basis of his research. As late as 1984, the Hungarian mathematician Paul (Pál) Erdős (1913–96), one of the most prolific mathematicians in history, gave a seminar that consisted of a long list of unsolved problems arising in Euclidean geometry.

Most of the problems, solutions, and applications that have arisen during the centuries following the demise of the Greek mathematical tradition could not have been anticipated by the Greeks themselves. Their understanding of physics, logic, and mathematics was quite different from that of those who came after them. Our understanding and appreciation of their work, however, should also take into account the tremendous utility of the ideas they developed as well as their intrinsic beauty.

PART TWO

PROJECTIVE GEOMETRY

4

MATHEMATICS AND ART DURING THE RENAISSANCE

The next significant chapter in the history of geometry begins during the European Renaissance. The Renaissance began about 1,000 years after Pappus's death. One thousand years is, by most standards, a very long gap to leave in the history of anything, geometry included. These "lost" years belong to the medieval period of European history. Sometimes this period is called the Dark Ages, but that name applies to Europe alone. Elsewhere the situation was different. There were other cultures in other places that maintained a tradition of creative research into mathematics throughout this period. The reason for the gap in this history is that in this volume we are recounting the history of *geometry*, not mathematics in general, and there was not much innovation in geometry anywhere on Earth during the European Middle Ages. Again this is not to imply that the entire field of mathematics lay dormant while Europe, from a mathematical point of view, slept.

In what is now India, for example, mathematicians made one of the most important and far-reaching innovations in the history of mathematics. They incorporated a symbol for 0 into their system of numeration and devised a true place-value system of notation. Finally, accurate large-scale computations were practicable for the first time. The computations necessary for commerce and science were, with the help of the so-called Hindu system of numeration, finally easy enough to be done by the nonspecialist. The importance of this innovation cannot be overstated. Hindu mathematicians also contributed to the development of algebra, but they had little interest in geometry as a separate discipline. Nor was India the only place with a vigorous mathematical tradition during these centuries.

Islamic culture was in full flower and produced many fine mathematicians. Learning in general, and mathematics in particular,

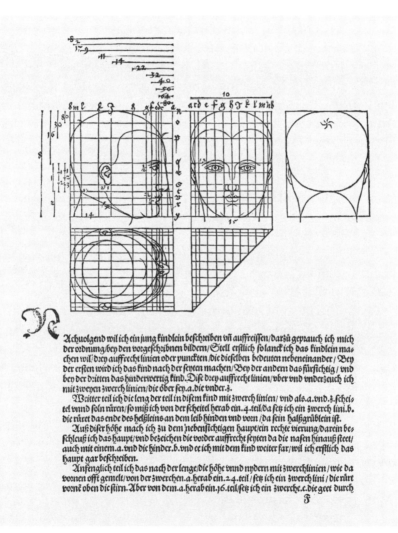

Drawings by Albrecht Dürer. The use of mathematical methods in the study of proportion and perspective was common practice among Renaissance artists. (Library of Congress, Prints and Photographs Division)

was emphasized in the Islamic world just as it was on the Indian subcontinent. Islamic mathematicians also preserved old knowledge by translating and circulating the works of their Greek predecessors. Many well-known ancient Greek texts are now known to us only through Arabic translations. Furthermore interaction between Islamic and Hindu mathematicians occurred during this time. Islamic mathematicians quickly recognized the importance of the system of numeration developed by Indian mathematicians. They translated some of the Indian texts into Arabic and quickly absorbed the place-value notation of their neighbors far to the east. In addition, Islamic mathematicians developed a new, rigorous approach to algebra. This, too, was an important innovation. All of this activity was important to the history of mathematics, but little of it added to the history of geometry.

The history of geometry resumes in the 15th century with the discovery of an entirely new geometry. This new geometry arose from the efforts of Renaissance-era artists to draw and paint the world as it appears to the eye, a type of art called representational art. Their innovations led to the development of the first of the non-Euclidean geometries. This new geometry is called projective geometry, and it is unique among all geometries because its origins lie in art rather than in science or mathematics.

To appreciate how projective geometry arose, it is helpful to recall what European art was like during the Middle Ages. Throughout the Middle Ages European artists strove to develop a rich visual language. Bible stories, especially those taken from the New Testament, formed the basis of many of their paintings. The religious scenes that they depicted are often easy to identify, and, indeed, communicating these stories to a largely illiterate populace was surely part of their aim. The central figures in these paintings are generally depicted with halos. Often the main characters in the story are painted much larger than the secondary characters. Sometimes the pictures depict the main characters out of proportion to the surrounding landscape as well, and the more important a character is to the story the closer he or she is to the center of the painting. The images can be very affecting. The composition of a painting, the use of color, the highly stylized imagery, and the evident passion of an often-anonymous artist make these pictures worthy of study, but to modern eyes the images also look stiff. There are no sense of motion and no feeling of lightness or heaviness. They have no sense of depth. There are no shadows, no apparent light sources, and no attempt at establishing a geometric perspective. These pictures have more in common with Egyptian hieroglyphics than they have with the style of painting that developed during the Renaissance. The recognition of the beauty present in these paintings is, for many of us, only the result of careful study. Medieval ideas of beauty are often far removed from our own.

One of the great triumphs of the Renaissance was the development of representational art. Some of the most prominent artists of the Renaissance remain household names in our own time. Even now many of us are familiar with the Italian artists Leonardo da Vinci, Michelangelo, and Raphael, and the German painter Albrecht Dürer. Each of these individuals created

The Lady of Kazan, *an example of nonrepresentational art. Notice, for example, that there are no clues that enable the viewer to determine whether or not the image of God in the clouds is small and situated near the foreground or large and situated far in the background. Notice, too, that the location of the light source that illuminates the faces of the main figures is not evident.* (Library of Congress, Prints and Photographs Division)

paintings that have resonated with viewers for hundreds of years. Today we remember these artists for their choice of subject matter and for the ideas that they communicated through their art. They are also remembered for their technical skill. The techniques that Renaissance artists employed were a vital part of what they accomplished artistically. Technique was important to them. Representational art was the goal of Renaissance artists, and they needed more than talent and a good eye to succeed in producing it.

The skills required to create a representational painting or drawing are not "natural." No one, howsoever talented, is born with these skills. Nor are we necessarily born with the desire to develop them. There is no evidence, for example, that the painters of medieval Europe were less talented than those who followed them. Nor is there any evidence that these nonrepresentational artists tried to develop representational techniques and failed. The techniques required to create representational art had to be invented, and the invention of these techniques occupied some of the best minds of the time. It is fortunate that some of the best artists of the Renaissance were also some of the best architects, scientists, mathematicians, and inventors of their period. They had the idea of creating representational art, and they had the skills necessary to discover a way to succeed.

Mathematically speaking the main difficulty in making representational art (and in what follows we restrict our attention to painting and drawing) is that the artist is striving to create a two-dimensional image of a three-dimensional object. As a consequence there is certain to be some distortion involved as the artist creates the flat image. Some Renaissance artists were well aware that *some* distortion is unpreventable. Their goal was not to eliminate distortion, but, instead, to find a rational way to *project* the image of a three-dimensional object onto a flat piece of canvas or paper so as to minimize the distortion involved. They soon recognized that there is a rational method for accomplishing this. A few artists also recognized that the method they used had a mathematical basis. Their search for the mathematical basis of these projection techniques marks the beginning of the development of *projective geometry*.

Leonardo da Vinci

The Italian artist, scientist, inventor, and architect Leonardo da Vinci (1452–1519) was educated as an artist. During Leonardo's life aspiring painters in Italy learned their craft as apprentices, and at about the age of 15 Leonardo was apprenticed to a prominent artist named Andrea del Verrocchio (1435–88). As a beginning apprentice Leonardo would have learned how to mix paints, stretch canvases, and acquire other basic "painterly" skills. As he got better he would have had the opportunity to finish paintings begun by the master. Eventually he would "graduate" by becoming a member of an artists' guild. In 1472 Leonardo was accepted into the painters' guild of Florence. At that time he could have begun work on his own, but he remained at Verrocchio's studio for an additional five years. This training had a pro-found effect on Leonardo. To the end of his life he identified himself as a painter even though he completed only a small number of pictures during his lifetime. In fact he refused many opportunities to paint and failed to complete many of the commissions that he accepted. Nevertheless it is clear from his writings that he considered painting to be an important discipline that offered one the opportunity to see more deeply into nature than one could see without studying painting. Today fewer than 20 of Leonardo's pictures remain.

When Leonardo was about 30 years old he began to study mathematics. He also began

Leonardo da Vinci's Mona Lisa. *Compare with* The Lady of Kazan *in the preceding section* (Library of Congress, Prints and Photographs Division)

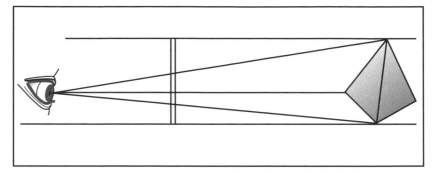

Leonardo's optical pyramid. The staff is used to investigate the shape of the pyramid.

to keep notebooks. Leonardo wrote regularly in notebooks for the rest of his life. The notebooks, which are our best source of information about Leonardo, are profusely illustrated and contain Leonardo's ideas about art, architecture, design, mathematics, numerous inventions, anatomy, physics, and a host of other subjects. Leonardo used his background as an artist to investigate all of these subjects. It is through his notebooks that we learn of Leonardo's ideas about the mathematical basis for representational painting and drawing.

Leonardo was not the first to notice that there is a mathematical basis to painting or drawing a scene in such a way that the three-dimensional scene appears on a surface in the same way that it appears to the eye. The Italian artists Leon Battista Alberti (1404–72) and Francesco della Pierro (ca. 1420–92) had already demonstrated that there was a mathematical basis for the techniques then in use, but Leonardo saw more deeply into the geometric ideas involved. Leonardo understood that visual images are transmitted through space along straight lines, and because every image must enter our pupils to be seen, the images have to form what Leonardo called "pyramids." "The eye sees in no other way than by a pyramid," he tells us, but these are not pyramids in the usual sense. The vertex, or point, of the pyramid is a point just inside the pupil of our eye. The base of the pyramid is the outline of the object that the observer sees. When we see a round object, for example, the base of Leonardo's optical pyramid is round. When we see a dog, the base of the pyramid is in the shape of a dog. The lines that make up the sides of the pyramid converge toward a point just behind the pupil of the observer.

The idea that we have optical pyramids extending into our pupils with bases formed by the objects around us, and the idea that these pyramids form each time we open our eyes, are admittedly unusual. Nevertheless they are very useful ideas if we want to understand how we perceive objects. For example, suppose we are looking at coins placed flat on a horizontal plane. Suppose we are standing on the plane so that our eyes are above it. The objects that are farther away appear higher up, and the farther away we place a coin the higher it appears. No matter how big the plane, however, no coin will ever appear to us to be higher than the horizon. This observation explains why more distant objects are generally drawn so as to appear closer to the top of the painting.

Leonardo also uses this idea to explain why objects that are farther away appear smaller. The farther away an object is placed, the smaller the angle formed by the optical pyramid with that object as base. To investigate this phenomenon further Leonardo suggests holding a staff upright at various distances from the eye (see the diagram). Notice that the farther from the eye we place the staff, the narrower the pyramid formed by the ends of the staff and our pupil. The rate at which the angle at the apex diminishes as the base of the pyramid is moved farther away can be measured. Leonardo suggests an experiment involving a staff and a tower. Place the staff vertically between the eye and the tower so that the ends of the staff appear to coincide with the bottom and top of the tower. Now move the staff horizontally toward the observer. As the staff moves toward the observer the top of the staff appears to extend above the top of the tower, and simultaneously the bottom of the staff appears to extend below the bottom of the tower. Marks on the staff can be used to show that Leonardo's optical pyramid is, in fact, pyramidal in shape.

These observations are what one needs to draw a representational picture of an object or a scene. To render a representational drawing or painting all that is necessary is to imagine a pane of glass between the object and the artist. The pane of glass cuts the optical pyramid along a flat surface. The job of the artist is then to paint or draw what appears on the glass. There is, however, more than one way to position the glass so that it cuts the pyramid. We can place the glass closer to the eye or farther away. We can tilt the glass up or down, left or right. In each case the image that appears on the glass changes: That is, our sense of perspective changes. If we only move the glass back and forth the distances between various parts of the image change. If we tilt the glass, the angle formed between the glass and the sides of the pyramid also changes. When this occurs, the angles that make up the image on the glass change as well. As a consequence, Leonardo's method for generating a perspective drawing preserves neither distances nor angles. This is not a mistake. As we change position relative to a fixed object, angles and distances *do* change. It is unpreventable. Nevertheless, in every case if we follow Leonardo's model, the drawing is "in perspective" for that particular position of the observer's eye and that particular orientation of the pane of glass.

Leonardo's optical pyramid is not an exact model of the way we actually see the world around us. Leonardo acknowledges as much in his writing. He points out that his model is a good representation for the way we see with one eye. With two eyes—as most of us see the world—the situation is more complicated. His model does not account for some of the phenomena that arise when we look around us with both eyes. For example, if we place the side of a hand between the eyes and along the nose, one eye sees one side of the hand and the other eye sees the other side of the hand. Leonardo's model for vision does not take this effect into account.

Another consequence of Leonardo's model is that our view of a painting is distorted if we stand in the wrong place to observe it. For example, suppose that from the artist's perspective a sphere appears on the plate of glass as a circle. The artist then draws the sphere as a circle, but if we stand off to the side of the picture to observe it, then *from our perspective* the artist's circle looks like an ellipse. In this case although the artist painted the object correctly, our view of the "correct" image is distorted by the position from which we view it. Leonardo suggests that to evaluate the technique of an artist properly we need to stand in the proper place and look at the painting through one eye. From a practical point of view, however, the real difficulty with Leonardo's approach is that there is in general no practical way to connect his imaginary plane of glass with the painting we may wish to produce.

Albrecht Dürer

Albrecht Dürer (1471–1528) was as well known and as much admired in Germany and the Low Countries as Leonardo was in Italy and France. Dürer's first teacher was his father, who was a goldsmith by trade. At the age of 15 Dürer was apprenticed to the painter and printmaker Michael Wolgemut (1434–1519). By 1490 Dürer was finished with his apprenticeship and ready to begin a lifetime in the pursuit of art.

Unlike Leonardo, Dürer was prolific. In addition to creating paintings, Dürer was a successful engraver and a theoretician. He wrote a four-volume work, *Course in the Art of Measurement*, about the importance of geometry and measurement in representational art. It is a mixed collection of results, but the general emphasis is on the application of mathematics to problems in perspective. Interestingly in *Course in the Art of Measurement* Dürer also demonstrates an interest in classical Greek geometry. He writes, for example, about the problem of doubling a cube, one of the three unsolved problems of classical geometry, and he demonstrates a familiarity with conic sections, although he is clearly more interested in finding rational ways of drawing them than in discovering their deeper mathematical properties. Dürer's motivation for his mathematical writings was to analyze and make accessible to his contemporaries in Northern Europe the theory behind the art that was being created primarily in Southern Europe by Leonardo and others. The Renaissance arrived late in Northern Europe.

It is clear from Dürer's writings that he did not consider math and art to be mutually exclusive subject areas. Math, to Dürer, was more than a tool. It was something he enjoyed. He even included mathematical themes in some of his paintings, but his theoretical conclusions about perspective were not much deeper, mathematically speaking, than Leonardo's. What is different is that Dürer showed how to make a practical, though extremely laborious, device to implement his (and Leonardo's) ideas about perspective. Essentially Dürer tells us how to construct what we would now

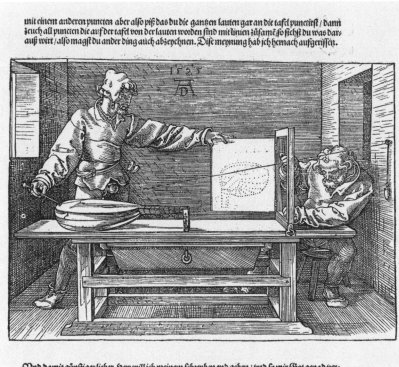

Albrecht Dürer's device for creating a sense of perspective in a picture (Library of Congress, Prints and Photographs Division)

call a projection—and what Leonardo imagined as a pane of glass—between the observer and the object. This device allows the user to produce a practical demonstration of the techniques of perspective drawing. It is a remarkable invention that is based on several important geometrical ideas. We have included Dürer's own picture of the device, which was originally created in the form of a woodcut, as a reference.

Dürer begins by identifying the apex and base of the optical pyramid. In his example the base is the lute and the apex is the eyelet attached to the wall on the right side of the illustration. If we could place an eye at the eyelet and attempt to draw the lute as it appears from the eyelet, we would encounter a technical challenge. The difficulty arises from the position of the lute. The neck of the lute is pointed toward the observer. As a result the body and neck of the lute appear severely foreshortened in any drawing that we render from our position at the eyelet. Dürer's device helps the artist visualize the lute from the point of view of the eyelet. This is important because his purely mechanical device enables the artist to "cut" the optical pyramid that has its base at the lute and apex at the eyelet in a way that Leonardo's concept of a pane of glass could not. Even better Dürer's invention enables the artist to see the results.

The first step in using this device is for the artist to erect a frame with a door that can be opened and closed. On the back of the door the artist collects what we might call "data points" for the lute. (Dürer, of course, would have called them no such thing.) The frame, with the door opened, corresponds to the pane of glass that Leonardo imagined using to cut the optical pyramid. The mathematical term for this pane of glass is a *section*.

String is used to make the sides of the optical pyramid visible. The person on the left uses a pointer with the string tied at one end. The pointer is used to select a spot on the lute for analysis. The other end of the string loops through the eyelet on the right. A weight is tied onto the string beneath the eyelet to keep it taut. If we imagine the observer's eye at the eyelet then the string shows us the path that the ray of light travels from a point on the lute to the observer's eye.

To help us visualize the image that the rays of light make on the section, Dürer uses two more strings: a taut vertical string, parallel to the vertical sides of the frame, and a taut horizontal string that is parallel to the horizontal sides of the frame. The vertical string can be moved back and forth along the frame and the horizontal string can be moved up and down along the frame. Here is how the device works:

STEP 1: The person on the left of the drawing places the pointer at a point on the lute whose projection we wish to investigate. In so doing, she or he creates a line (the string) from the point on the lute to the eyelet.

STEP 2: The person on the right moves the two strings on the rectangular frame until they cross at the point where the line pierces the section, which is represented by the frame.

STEP 3: The perspective line is withdrawn from the frame and the door on the frame is closed. The two strings on the frame now mark a point on the door, which the person on the right marks.

This procedure is repeated as often as desired. The result is a collection of dots that, if connected, enable the user to visualize how the lute looks from the perspective of the eyelet. Notice that the collection of dots on the door in the illustration form a nice outline of the foreshortened lute.

This is a beautiful math experiment to demonstrate the geometry of perspective, and the device is a concrete representation of certain fundamental ideas in a branch of mathematics that would later be known as projective geometry.

The search for a mathematical basis for the techniques of representational art was an important first step in the development of projective geometry. These artists provided a context for further study as well as the first concrete examples of projections. Although they proved no theorems, their work provided the basis for more rigorous mathematical inquiries in much the same way that Egyptian surveying techniques are said to have inspired the Greeks to begin their study of geometry.

This is not to say that these artists "reduced" their art to a series of mathematical rules. The writings that they and their contemporaries left behind make it clear that they were fully engaged in an artistic process. They sought to communicate emotions and aesthetic values through their art. It would be a mistake to believe otherwise. But it is also an error to fail to see that this style of art has a mathematical basis and that some of the most important of these artists knew that their art was founded on mathematical principles, and that they believed that their artistic efforts were most successful when they took place in a mathematical context.

These works of art have inspired art lovers the world over. They also inspired a very creative 17th-century mathematician to attempt to develop a new branch of geometry that would express and extend the mathematical insights of these artists in a more rigorous and logically satisfactory way.

5

THE FIRST THEOREMS

A theorem is a statement that is not self-evident and that has been *proved* true. Neither Leonardo nor Dürer produced a single theorem in the field of projective geometry. It is true that they recognized some of the basic concepts of this branch of mathematics. We can read in their words the ideas that would eventually constitute some of the axioms of this new branch of thought, but neither Leonardo nor Dürer had the background necessary to place these concepts in a rigorous mathematical context. The first person to turn the work of the artists of the Renaissance into a collection of mathematical theorems was the French mathematician Gérard (also known as Gaspard or Girard) Desargues (1591–1661).

In addition to being interested in mathematics, Gérard Desargues was an engineer and architect. In these capacities he worked for the French government. He loved mathematics and he knew many of the best mathematicians of his time. Desargues was one of the fortunate few mathematicians of his time who had the opportunity to attend weekly meetings at the home of the French priest Marin Mersenne (1588–1648). Father Mersenne made his home a place where the best mathematicians in Paris could gather to trade ideas and to learn. Because there were no scholarly journals, these clubs—there were similar clubs in other cities—together with regular correspondence, were the means mathematicians and scientists used to communicate their discoveries. It was at these meetings that Desargues described his ideas for a new geometry based on the techniques of Renaissance artists.

Desargues's ideas were not well received. Part of the problem was that Desargues expressed his new ideas in a new mathematical vocabulary. He invented this vocabulary specifically to express these ideas; that was unfortunate, because as a general rule it is hard to convince most people to learn an entirely new vocabulary just to evaluate a set of ideas that may or may not be worth considering. Furthermore Desargues wrote in a very terse style that many people apparently found difficult to read. Matters of style and vocabulary aside, however, Desargues's ideas about geometry were highly original. This difference alone would have made Desargues's geometry difficult to appreciate even under the best of circumstances.

To appreciate the conceptual difficulties involved in understanding this new geometry, recall that a projection of an image usually changes both the angles and lengths one finds in the image. (This is often expressed by saying that projections preserve neither lengths nor angular measurements.) Desargues's contemporaries, however, were familiar only with Euclidean geometry, and lengths and angular measurements are the currency of Euclidean geometry. They are exactly what mathematicians study when they study this geometry. But Desargues's projections destroyed exactly those properties that his contemporaries recognized as geometric. The first question, then, was whether there was anything left to study in Desargues's new geometry: What, if any, properties remained the same from one projection to the next? Desargues needed to identify interesting properties that are *preserved* under projections, because those are the properties that must form the basis of the subject. Because Desargues had already eliminated lengths and angles as objects of study, it was not immediately clear whether he had left himself anything to study.

The property of being a triangle is preserved under a projection. Although neither the shape nor the size of the triangle is preserved, the image of any triangle under a projection is always another triangle. Unfortunately this observation is almost self-evident. What Desargues wanted to identify were other, deeper properties that might be preserved under projections. From an artistic point of view, there is good reason to suspect that many properties are preserved by projections. Two distinct projections are, after all, alternate images of the same object. It seems at least

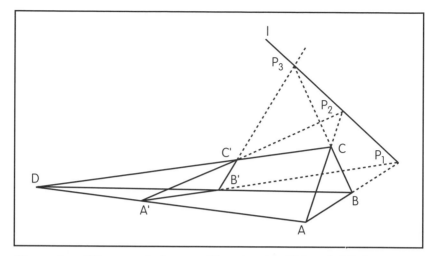

Illustration of Desargues's theorem. The triangles ABC and A'B'C' and the point D are assumed given and the existence of the line l must be proved.

plausible that there would exist other, more interesting properties that all projections of the same image would have in common.

Desargues's first paper, *Treatise on the Perspective Section*, contains what is now called Desargues's theorem. It is one of the most famous theorems in projective geometry, in part because it is the first theorem, and in part because it shows the existence of a nonobvious property of a *projective transformation*. To follow the description of Desargues's theorem, refer to the accompanying diagram. Notice that triangles *ABC* and *A'B'C'* are "in perspective": That is, each triangle is a section of the same optical pyramid so that *A'* is the image of *A* under the projection, *B'* is the image of *B*, and *C'* the image of *C*. Desargues's theorem states that if we extend corresponding sides of each triangle, not only will the corresponding sides intersect, but also all three points of intersection, which we have marked as P_1, P_2, and P_3, will lie on the same line. With one important exception, this is true no matter how we project our triangle *ABC*.

The exception to Desargues's theorem arises—or at least seems to arise—when the section that determines triangle *A'B'C'* is chosen so that one or more sides of the two triangles are parallel with one another. If the corresponding sides of the triangles are parallel then they do not intersect in the ordinary Euclidean sense. The solution to the problem of parallel lines is to define them out of existence. Here is how this is done: We assume the existence of an extra point, the *point at infinity*—which is defined so that the "parallel" lines intersect at this extra point. Now we can say that *in all cases* the three points that result from the intersection of corresponding lines are collinear: That is, the three points lie on one and the same line.

The existence of the extra point at infinity may seem artificial, but it turns out to be a tremendous convenience. Furthermore although it may sound strange to say that two parallel lines intersect at the point at infinity, the phrase simply echoes what we observe in any picture that purports to represent two parallel lines receding toward the horizon. The two lines always converge to a single point located on the horizon of the picture. The difference between the language of projective geometry and the language of representational art is that in art the point at infinity is called a vanishing point. The vanishing point is the point where the two parallel lines appear to meet. In projective geometry "the vanishing point" is simply called the point at infinity. Desargues's theorem is an important example of a nonobvious property that a triangle and its projection share. Here is a more formal statement of Desargues's theorem:

> Given two triangles, if the lines determined by the pairs of corresponding vertices all meet at a common point, then the points determined by corresponding sides all lie along a common line.

For Desargues this was just the beginning. After discovering the theorem that bears his name, he turned his attention away from simple triangles and toward conic sections. He wanted to know which properties of a conic section, if any, were preserved under a projection. His discovery is contained in his masterpiece *Proposed Draft of an Attempt to Deal with the Events of the Meeting of a Cone with a Plane*. Desargues investigates the same conic sections that Apollonius investigated almost 2,000 years earlier. The difference is that Desargues treats them from *his* point of view, the point of view of projective geometry. In doing so, he discovers something startling about the nature of conic sections: No matter how a conic section is projected, the result is another conic section. The image of an ellipse under a projection need not be an ellipse. Under a projection the image of an ellipse may, for example, be a parabola or it may be a hyperbola. It may be a differently shaped ellipse as well. The image of an ellipse under a projection depends on the way we choose the section. What Desargues showed is that the image of an ellipse *must* be (1) another ellipse, (2) a parabola, or (3) a hyperbola. *No other possibilities exist.* Furthermore what has been said of an ellipse can equally accurately be said of a parabola and a hyperbola. A projection of a conic section is always a conic section, and it is in this sense that all conics are "the same" in projective geometry.

As Desargues developed his new geometry and described his ideas at the home of Marin Mersenne, the future French philosopher Blaise Pascal (1623–62), then a 16-year-old, became inspired by Desargues's work. Pascal attended the weekly meetings at the home of Marin Mersenne along with his father, Etienne Pascal. Etienne was a mathematician with very clear ideas about education. It was he who taught his son. Etienne, in fact, taught Blaise all the basic subjects except math, the teaching of which he intended to postpone until his son was 15 years old. As a consequence all mathematics books were removed from the Pascal home. By the age of 12, however, Blaise had begun to study mathematics unassisted. When he discovered that the sum of the measures of the interior angles of a triangle equals the sum of two right angles (the proof of which is to be found in chapter 2 of this volume), his father gave him a copy of Euclid's *Elements*. From that time onward Etienne encouraged Blaise in his study of mathematics.

Blaise turned out to be a prodigy, and of all the mathematicians exposed to the work of Desargues, the young Pascal was one of the very few who grasped its importance. Soon Blaise was busy searching for other properties of geometric figures that were invariant under projections. He found one. His discovery, which relates hexagons and conic sections, was an important insight into projective geometry. He published it under the title *Essay on Conics*. This theorem is now called Pascal's theorem. Essentially we can express Pascal's theorem in five brief statements (see the accompanying diagram):

- Suppose we have a conic section.
- Choose six points that lie on this conic.
- Connect the six points so as to form a hexagon. (The hexagon is a very general type of hexagon. It has six vertices, but it usually does not resemble the familiar regular hexagon.)
- Extend each pair of opposite sides of the hexagon until they intersect.
- The three points of intersection will lie on a single line.

To do Pascal's theorem full justice would require a much longer description. Because opposite sides of even an irregular hexagon may be parallel, we need to introduce the point at infinity again, just as we did for Desargues's theorem, in order to state his idea with precision. This, however, would take us too far afield, so we forgo the technical niceties. Pascal's theorem, as Desargues's theorem did, pointed the way to a new type of geometry, but for a long time neither Desargues's work nor Pascal's attracted much attention.

Pascal's theorem is one-half of an extraordinary discovery. How much Pascal understood about the implications of his own discovery is not clear. Pascal wrote a longer work that extended his ideas about

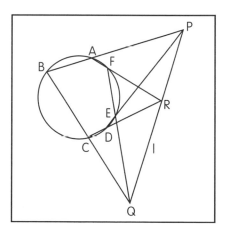

Illustration for Pascal's theorem. The hexagon ABCDEF is inscribed in the conic. The pairs of opposite sides are AB and DE, AF and CD, EF and BC. Extending these sides determines the three points P, R, and Q that are contained on line l.

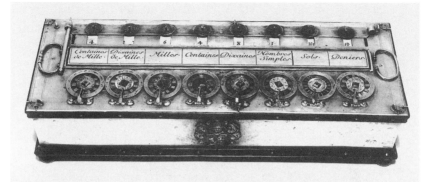

The Pascaline, the first working mechanical calculator (Courtesy of IBM Corporate Archives)

projective geometry, but this work was never published and is now lost. It would be well over a century before Pascal's theorem was rediscovered and generalized by the French mathematician Charles Jules Brianchon.

With the work of these two highly creative mathematicians, Desargues and Pascal, projective geometry was off to a promising start. Unfortunately their discoveries were, for the most part, ignored. Desargues's discoveries were so far from the mainstream of mathematics at the time that some people ridiculed his work. Only René Descartes, Desargues's friend and himself a prominent mathematician, offered any encouragement. Worse, Desargues was soon working alone again, because although Pascal was very imaginative, his interests changed as often as the weather. By the age of 18 Pascal was busy designing and constructing one of the first mechanical calculators in history.

Desargues's ideas were ahead of what most mathematicians of the time were prepared to imagine. His *Proposed Draft of an Attempt to Deal with the Events of the Meeting of a Cone with a Plane* was printed in 1639 and soon forgotten. All copies were lost and all knowledge of Desargues's treatise was restricted to a single manuscript copy. In the early years of the 19th century, however, as mathematicians again began to ask and answer the same questions that Desargues had grappled with 150 years earlier,

MARIN MERSENNE

The French priest Marin Mersenne (1588–1648) is a prominent figure in the history of mathematics. He was a talented mathematician, who enjoyed studying the theory of numbers and discovered a class of prime numbers that are now called Mersenne primes. In addition to his own research into mathematics he took an active interest in all matters scientific and mathematical. Father Mersenne was a strong proponent of rational thought. He strongly supported research in science and mathematics, and he spoke out against the pseudosciences of alchemy and astrology. Further Mersenne acted as a link between many of the most prominent scientists and mathematicians of the time. He traveled widely and maintained an extensive correspondence with many well-known scientists and mathematicians, including René Descartes, Galileo Galilei, and Pierre de Fermat. When scientists and mathematicians informed Mersenne of their discoveries he passed the news along. This was a very important and time-consuming activity. Recall that at the time there were no scientific journals. Father Mersenne's letters provided an important link, perhaps the most important link, connecting many of the great thinkers of Europe. Moreover he held weekly meetings at his home that attracted many of the best mathematicians in Paris. It was there that ideas were exchanged and debated. The letters exchanged between Marin Mersenne and his friends, as well as the weekly get-togethers at his home, had a profound impact on the development of mathematics in the 17th century.

Desargues's work finally began to attract the attention that it deserved. His ideas were expanded into an entire branch of geometry that attracted the attention of some of the best mathematicians of the time. By the beginning of the 20th century projective geometry had begun to fade from view again because many of the most important questions had been resolved, but Desargues could not be forgotten. Amazingly after centuries in obscurity a single original, printed copy of *Proposed Draft of an Attempt to Deal with the Events of the Meeting of a Cone with a Plane* was rediscovered in 1951. In 1964 a crater on the Moon was named after Desargues.

Today, Desargues's ideas are often taught to college undergraduates enrolled in introductory "modern" geometry courses. Furthermore, all mathematicians now have at least passing familiarity with the concepts of projective geometry. Probably Desargues would have taken some satisfaction in this turn of events, but he probably would have found it even more satisfying had his ideas received half as much attention while he was still alive. His ideas have not changed, of course. His theorems are the same now as they were then. Rather, society has finally caught up, and we are now in the position to enjoy mathematical ideas that impress many of us as beautiful but not especially exotic. Desargues's highly original ideas were far ahead of his time. He is the first geometer in this narrative to suffer neglect because he saw farther than his contemporaries, but we will soon see that his experience was by no means unique.

6

PROJECTIVE GEOMETRY REDISCOVERED

The ideas of Desargues lay dormant for about 150 years. Initially, many mathematicians were busy inventing the subject that would lead to the calculus. Calculus is part of a branch of mathematics called analysis. Almost from the start the results obtained with the new analysis were useful in the sense that they found immediate application in science and mathematics. Consequently this new branch of thought attracted the attention of many, perhaps most, of the best mathematicians of the era. The field of geometry entered a period of dormancy. Analysis was used to describe the motion of planets, the motions of fluids, and the mystery of ocean tides. The discovery of the field of analysis changed everything. For a while most mathematical research was research into analysis. In particular the ideas of Desargues and the young Pascal were largely forgotten.

The story of projective geometry resumes in the work of the French mathematician Gaspard Monge (1746–1818). Monge led a frantic, breathless life. He was interested in many branches of science as well as mathematics. He was ambitious and impossibly hardworking, and his life was greatly complicated by the political turmoil that occurred in France during his lifetime.

Monge was born into a France that was ruled by aristocrats. He showed mathematical promise early in life. As a teenager he developed his own ideas about geometry, but because his father was a merchant, he found himself working as a draftsman at Ecole Militaire de Mézières, an institution where the best places were

Rioting during the French Revolution, 1789. The French Revolution profoundly affected the lives of many of the best mathematicians of the time. (Library of Congress, Prints and Photographs Division)

reserved for the sons of aristocrats. When Monge was asked to determine gun emplacements for a proposed fortress, he saw an opportunity to use his geometric ideas. The standard method of determining gun emplacements at the time involved numerous time-consuming arithmetic calculations. Using his own geometric methods Monge solved the problem so quickly that at first his solution was not accepted. After further reflection the authorities accepted Monge's ideas. They also classified his geometric method as a military secret. Soon Monge was offered a position as a teacher rather than as a draftsman. Monge was on his way up.

Monge's ideas about geometry included ideas about shadows and perspective, and he is credited with developing a type of mathematics called descriptive geometry. (Descriptive geometry has some ideas in common with projective geometry.) But Monge's interests extended far beyond geometry. He also wrote about mathematical analysis, chemistry, optics, meteorology, metallurgy, educational reform, and other topics besides. He was indefatigable. Within a few years of becoming a teacher at Ecole Militaire de Mézières Monge had accepted a second, simultaneous position teaching at the Académie des Sciences in Paris. When scheduling conflicts arose he used his own money to hire someone to teach in his place at one of the institutions. Eventually Monge would accept still a third simultaneous position as examiner of naval cadets. It was also during this time that he helped to establish the metric system in France. As a scientist Monge was interested in theory and experiment, and he contributed to the development of both.

Monge's ideas about geometry were very inclusive. His class in what he called descriptive geometry included chapters on the study of surfaces, shadows, topography, perspective, and other subjects. He used his insight into geometry to develop what later became known as mechanical drawing, the mechanical representation of three-dimensional objects via perpendicular, two-dimensional sections. Monge believed that geometry was in many ways more fundamental than the field of mathematical analysis. In fact he used what are now known as geometrical methods to express and solve problems in analysis. It is through Monge's work that geometry again assumed a central place in the field of mathematics.

When the French Revolution began, Monge supported the revolutionaries. It was a dangerous time. There was turmoil within France and at the borders between France and its neighbors. The spirit of the times is apparent in his evolving research interests. Monge wrote about manufacturing cannons and explosives. He wrote about foundry work. He also continued to teach. As we shall soon see, it was through his teaching that, in the end, Monge had his greatest effect on the history of geometry.

The French Revolution was eventually subverted, and France was put under the rule of Napoléon Bonaparte (1769–1821), the French military and political leader. Monge and Napoléon became fast friends. (Napoléon was very interested in mathematics.) During this time Monge traveled frequently. He was sent to Italy by Napoléon to help identify art treasures that the French could take for their own. He accompanied Napoléon to Egypt.

Later when Napoléon's fortunes took a turn for the worse, Monge had to run for his life. After Napoléon was discredited, the new government stripped Monge of the honors that had been bestowed upon him by previous French governments, and he was thereafter excluded from French scientific life. He died a few years later.

Monge's Students

Monge's influence on mathematics was felt for many years through his pupils. The French mathematician and teacher Charles-Jules Brianchon (1785–1864) was a student of Monge. As Monge's was, Brianchon's personal life was profoundly affected by the turmoil of the times. After completing his formal education Brianchon served in the French army as an artillery officer in Spain and Portugal. Eventually his health took a turn for the worse and he retired from the service. He settled into teaching. For a while after he found work as a teacher he continued to do research in mathematics. Still later he turned his attention toward chemistry. Brianchon's mathematical output was not large.

While Brianchon was a student he discovered a remarkable theorem that is closely related to Pascal's theorem. It is for this theorem that Brianchon is best remembered. As were most mathematicians of the time Brianchon was unaware of Pascal's work in projective geometry. As a consequence he began his research by rediscovering Pascal's theorem. He then went on to prove his own theorem, a theorem that has a peculiar symmetry with Pascal's theorem. (A picture illustrating the content of Pascal's theorem is to be found on page 68.) Here are the two theorems compared:

Pascal's theorem:

> Given a hexagon inscribed within a conic section, the points of intersection of opposite sides of the hexagon are contained on a single line.

Brianchon's theorem:

> Given a hexagon circum-
> scribed about a conic section,
> lines connecting opposite
> vertices of the hexagon
> intersect at a single point.

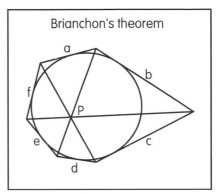

Brianchon's theorem. Hexagon abcdef is circumscribed about the conic section. When opposite vertices of the hexagon are joined by lines, all three lines intersect at the same point P.

Notice that Brianchon's theorem is essentially Pascal's theorem with the following substitutions: (1) *line* is interchanged with *point*, (2) *sides* is interchanged with *vertices* (which is just another line–point substitution), (3) *circumscribed* is interchanged with *inscribed*, and (4) *contained on* is interchanged with *intersect at.* All of these substitutions simply involve interchanging words that describe points with those that describe lines. (Even the circumscribed–inscribed substitution can be understood in this way.) Notice, too, that if we begin with Brianchon's theorem instead of Pascal's theorem, then we can obtain Pascal's theorem by making the appropriate substitutions.

Pascal's theorem and Brianchon's theorem are, in a sense, two sides of the same mathematical coin. Projective geometry was not yet sufficiently understood to make full use of this observation, but Brianchon had discovered an early instance of what would later be known as the principle of duality. It is to the discoverer of the principle of duality, a remarkable and fundamental idea in projective geometry, that we now turn our attention.

Jean-Victor Poncelet (1788–1867) was another of Monge's students and also a friend of Brianchon. (Poncelet and Brianchon wrote a mathematics paper together.) As Monge's and Brianchon's were, Poncelet's life was in many ways determined by the turmoil that engulfed France. After his student years Poncelet became a military engineer in Napoléon's army. He served under Napoléon during the invasion of Russia. For the French army, the invasion of Russia was a disaster. The French not only were defeated, but suffered very high casualties. Remnants of the French army managed to return to France, but many were left behind. Jean-Victor Poncelet was one of those who remained in Russia. Left for dead, he spent the next two years in a Russian prison, and it was during this time that he studied projective geometry. His contributions to projective geometry so far exceeded those of Desargues, Pascal, Brianchon, and others that he is sometimes described as having founded the subject.

Prisons, especially those built for prisoners of war, have a reputation for being harsh environments. The prisons in czarist Russia were no exception. Nevertheless Poncelet thrived in the harsh environment. During the two years that he was imprisoned in Russia, Poncelet managed to do enough mathematics to produce a two-volume work, *Applications of Analysis and Geometry*, which was intended to serve as an introduction to another work, *Treatise on the Projective Properties of Figures*. Poncelet's plans did not unfold smoothly after his term as a prisoner was completed. The *Treatise*, which turned out to be the work for which Poncelet is best remembered, was written after he returned to France in 1814. It was published in 1822. Its introduction, *Applications of Analysis and Geometry*, was eventually published in sections 40 years later during the years 1862 to 1864.

Poncelet is often called "the father of projective geometry" because it is in Poncelet's work that many of the most important concepts of projective geometry first appear. It was Poncelet who first identified many of the most important characteristics of figures that are preserved under projections. Included in his discoveries was the very important concept of cross-ratio.

As its name implies, the cross-ratio is a ratio, but a peculiar kind of ratio. We already know that distances are not preserved under projections. It was probably something of a surprise to these early mathematicians that in addition ratios of distances are not preserved. The ratio AB/BC is *not* equal to the ratio $A'B'/B'C'$. What is preserved under projections is *the ratio of the ratios* of the distances, so that the cross-ratio of four points after a projection is the same as the cross-ratio before the projection (refer to the following diagram).

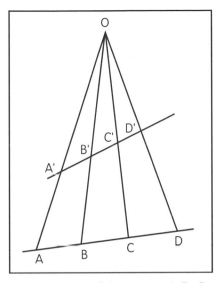

The importance of the cross-ratio stems from the following essential fact: Any transformation of space that preserves the cross-ratio is a projective transformation. In other words, the concepts of cross-ratio and projection are intimately related. Additionally the cross-ratio can be used to understand how the positions of points change under projections.

The projection of the points, A, B, C, and D onto the points A′, B′, C′, and D′ preserves the cross-ratio.

The cross-ratio is determined by the following formula:

$$\frac{\frac{AC}{CB}}{\frac{AD}{DB}} = \frac{\frac{A'C'}{C'B'}}{\frac{A'D'}{D'B'}}$$

The only additional restriction is that the lengths represented by the pairs of letters represent *directed* lengths: If we take the direction from *A* to *C* as positive then the segment *AC* is a positive length and the segment *DB* is a negative one.

This, at least, was the original conception of cross-ratios. Later it was discovered that one did not need to know anything at all about the distances between the four points to know about their cross-ratio. In projective geometry definitions and ideas that do not depend on distances play a special role, because (again) in projective geometry distance is not a "geometric property." The fact that Poncelet still used distances to define projective concepts indicates that he had not quite freed himself from the ideas of Euclidean geometry. He still saw Euclidean geometry as the more fundamental of the two geometries, but further research would soon indicate otherwise.

Poncelet also discovered a wonderful and surprising property of projective geometry called the principle of duality. We have already encountered an example of duality in our discussion of Pappus's theorem and in Brianchon's theorem. In both instances we saw that if we interchange the words *line* and *point* in each theorem and make a few other changes in the grammar, we obtain a new and true statement. In projective geometry this surprising property—that we can simply interchange the words *point* and *line* in one theorem to get a new and true statement—is quite general. Each time one statement is proved true, another true statement can be obtained simply by interchanging the words *point* and *line* and adjusting the grammar. When one statement is true, both statements are true. For example, here is Desargues's theorem along with its dual:

Desargues's theorem:

> Given two triangles, if the lines determined by the pairs of corresponding vertices all meet at a common point, then the points determined by corresponding sides all lie along a common line.

The dual of Desargues's theorem reads as follows:

> Given two triangles, if the points determined by the pairs of corresponding sides all meet on a common line, then the lines determined by the corresponding vertices all intersect at a common point.

Both statements are true. The discovery of the duality principle in projective geometry led to a flurry of new theorems as mathematicians simply looked at old theorems—theorems that had been previously proved true—and rewrote them, interchanging the words *point* and *line* and correcting the grammar of the result. It was that easy.

The existence of the duality principle was something of a surprise. There is not, for example, a duality principle in Euclidean geometry, although we can find isolated dual statements, such as the theorem of Pappus. In Euclidean geometry when we interchange the words *line* and *point* we generally get a false statement. For example, although it is true that in Euclidean geometry any two points determine a line, it is, in general, false that any two lines determine a point. (The exception occurs when the lines are parallel.)

Poncelet was not the only mathematician to take credit for discovering the principle of duality. Another student of Monge's, the French mathematician and soldier Joseph Diaz Gergonne (1771–1859), also claimed to have discovered the principle of duality. Gergonne's father, like some of the Renaissance artists who began to investigate the foundations of projective geometry, was a painter and architect. He died when Gergonne was 12. Gergonne displayed a lifelong interest in mathematics, but as so many citizens of France did, he spent much of his early adulthood participating in military campaigns. As Brianchon did, Gergonne served in Spain. In the end Gergonne settled down to study mathematics and write about his discoveries. In publishing his ideas, however, Gergonne had an advantage over most mathematicians of his time. He had his own mathematical journal. Although he originally called it *Annales de mathématique pures et appliqués*, it came to be known as *Annales de Gergonne*. The ideas of many of the best French mathematicians of the time were published in the *Annales*. Brianchon and Poncelet, for example, had some of their work published in Gergonne's journal.

There was some competition between Gergonne and Poncelet. In addition to the dispute about which of them had discovered the principle of duality, they had competing ideas about the best way to express geometry. Poncelet favored what is called synthetic geometry, a method devoid of algebraic symbolism. Greek geometry is often described as synthetic. Notice, for example, that in chapter 2 in the proof that the sum of the interior angles of a triangle equals the sum of two right angles, there is no algebra. Monge, too, sometimes used synthetic methods. This type of reasoning fell out of favor with the rise of analysis, but it was used again in the first half of the 19th century. Gergonne thought that geometric truths were best expressed in the language of algebra. That is, he favored analytic methods.

Though their competing visions and claims seemed to start off amicably enough, the disputes between Poncelet and Gergonne eventually became bitter. In retrospect the discovery of the principle of duality may well have been one of those cases of simultaneous discovery, and it may not be fair to assign credit to one and not the other. But with respect to the question of whether synthetic or analytic methods facilitate discovery in geometry, the question (for now) has been largely resolved. Most mathematicians today prefer analytic methods.

Projective Geometry as a Mature Branch of Mathematics

For all their disagreements Poncelet and Gergonne both used measurement in their study of projective geometry. Though their ideas were in many ways new, they still saw projective geometry in terms of Euclidean geometry, in which the measurement of distances and angles is fundamental. But to really understand projective geometry and its place in mathematics, doing away with the concept of measurement entirely is helpful. This was the contribution of the German mathematician Karl Georg Christian von Staudt (1798–1867).

Unlike the French mathematicians Brianchon, Monge, Poncelet, and Gergonne, von Staudt led a quiet life. He was born and grew up in Rothenburg, Germany. As a young man he studied under Carl Friedrich Gauss, one of the most prolific mathematicians of the 19th century. Under Gauss von Staudt began his studies in astronomy, but he eventually turned his attention to geometry, especially projective geometry. Von Staudt's contribution to geometry was less a matter of technique and more a matter of philosophy. His accomplishment was to restate the ideas of projective geometry, including the concept of cross-ratio, in a way that was completely free of any reference to length. Essentially he showed that projective geometry is an independent branch of geometry. One did not need any results from Euclidean geometry to understand projective geometry. Projective geometry could be developed in a way that used none of the concepts of Euclid, Apollonius, and Archimedes.

Von Staudt's contribution was important because during the 19th century mathematicians were discovering numerous new geometries. They were discovering many, very different ways of thinking about points, lines, planes, and spaces. They had discovered that there is not one geometry but many geometries. The question that mathematicians then sought to resolve was how these diverse geometries were related. They wanted to know how much of each new geometry was really new and how much was simply a novel way of restating old ideas. Von Staudt's work demonstrated that projective geometry is really a new branch of geometry, not simply a peculiar way of looking at Euclidean concepts.

The ideas and techniques of projective geometry continued to draw the attention of leading mathematicians throughout the 19th century, but as the century drew to a close, interest in the subject began to wane. Perhaps the last great discovery about projective geometry made during the 19th century was due to the efforts of the German mathematician Felix Klein (1849–1925).

Felix Klein led the life of an academic. He was educated at the University of Bonn and after graduation moved several times to teach at different universities. Erlangen University and Göttingen University were among the places he worked. Klein was a highly imaginative mathematician with an interest in the big questions, and in the 19th century geometric questions were on the minds of many of the best mathematicians. The century saw the rise of numerous other geometries. Projective geometry attracted much of the attention, but as mathematicians realized that other, distinct geometries existed, they felt free to create and investigate geometries of their own invention. Geometry had fragmented. To an outsider it must have seemed a random collection of questions and answers. What, Klein asked, were the relationships among these geometries?

The concepts necessary to uncover the logical relationships between the different branches of geometry then known had already been developed decades earlier. The necessary ideas were not, however, part of geometry; they were part of algebra. As geometry was fragmenting, mathematicians had developed new conceptual tools to investigate the structure of mathematics. These new concepts were in the field of algebra. One such idea was the branch of mathematics now called group theory. It was with the help of group theory that Klein was able to reunify the field of geometry.

Beginning in the early 1800s the mathematicians Evariste Galois (1811–32) and Niels Henrik Abel (1802–29) developed a new way of thinking about mathematics. They began to recognize the existence of certain logical structures that are shared by very different-looking kinds of mathematics. They noticed that the same logical

The mathematics building at Göttingen University during the time of David Hilbert, Felix Klein, and Emmy Noether. For most of the 19th century and the first third of the 20th century, more of mathematics was discovered in this modest building than in any other place in the world. (Courtesy of University of Göttingen)

PROJECTIVE GEOMETRY TODAY

From the early 20th century onward there has not been much research into the foundations of projective geometry, but the field has not been entirely ignored. The University of Toronto has an excellent geometry department, and Donald Coxeter, an important 20th-century geometer at the University of Toronto, has obtained several interesting results about projective geometry. Still it is fair to say that since Klein's work, mathematicians have turned their attention elsewhere. Projective geometry is a mature subject. Most of the big theoretical questions in projective geometry have been answered for now, but that is not the end of projective geometry.

Late in the 20th century, mathematicians and computer programmers with a mathematical bent again became interested in projective geometry. They were interested in developing the computer programs necessary to represent three-dimensional objects on flat (two-dimensional) computer monitors. Representing a three-dimensional image on the surface of a monitor requires one to be able to project the image on the screen correctly. This is essentially the same problem faced by Renaissance artists. The difference is that the tool is not a paintbrush but a computer program. Their goals are to write the instructions necessary for the computer to represent a three-dimensional surface from a variety of viewpoints and for the result to resemble the given object. It is a problem with which Leonardo da Vinci and Albrecht Dürer would have been intimately familiar. It is also a nice example of how this mathematical problem has come full circle. Renaissance-era artists looked for a mathematical basis for the techniques that they were developing. Their goal was to find the mathematics necessary to represent a scene or object better. Now that the mathematics has been so fully developed, the goal is to write software that incorporates as much of the mathematics as necessary to represent three-dimensional objects on two-dimensional surfaces artistically.

Another application of projective geometry involves computer vision. Because the appearance of an object changes with the perspective of the observer, identifying an object from different positions depends on recognizing which properties remain invariant under a projective transformation. Interpreting the flat, pixilated computer images is facilitated by concepts from projective geometry. It has been 500 years since mathematicians began the search for the mathematical foundations of representational art. After all of this time, the concepts of projective geometry continue to fascinate the mathematically curious and help the artistically ambitious.

structures exist in arithmetic and analysis, geometry and algebra. The most prominent of these structures, the group, has proved to be a very useful tool in helping mathematicians understand how mathematics "works."

A *group* is a set of symbols that can be combined, subject to certain restrictions, to produce other symbols that are also in the group. Of course we can assign meanings to these symbols. We can say that the symbols represent numbers or geometric transformations, or we can give them some other interpretation. The interpretation that we place on the symbols depends on which questions we are asking and which objects we wish to study. But the interpretation of the symbols has no relation to the group. It is entirely possi-

GROUPS AND GEOMETRY

In mathematics a *group* is a collection of symbols and an operation. Sometimes a group is represented with a pair of symbols like this: $(G, \cdot)$. The letter G represents the set of objects. We can say that G is the set $\{a, b, c, \ldots\}$. The dot following G in $(G, \cdot)$ represents the operation we use to combine the objects. The group operation is somewhat analogous to multiplication. Every group satisfies four properties:

1. If a and b belong to G, then $a \cdot b$, the product of a and b, belongs to G.

2. If a, b, and c belong to G, then $(a \cdot b) \cdot c = a \cdot (b \cdot c)$: That is, we can combine a and b first and then combine c, or we can combine b and c first and then combine a; the result is the same.

3. Every group has one special element called the identity. It is usually represented with the letter e. The identity has the property that for any other element in G, $e \cdot a = a \cdot e = a$: That is, no matter how we combine e with a, where a represents any other element of G, the result is always a.

4. Finally, every element in G has an inverse: If a is any element of G, G must also contain another element called the inverse of a, written a^{-1}, with the property that $a \cdot a^{-1} = e$.

ble to study groups without giving any interpretation to the symbols. The exact definition of a group is not of immediate concern here. What is important is that there are certain criteria that every group satisfies, and that there are other criteria in which one group may differ from another. The differences between one group and another are what mathematicians use when they classify groups.

Klein's method was to examine the set of motions that is characteristic of each geometry. The set of all such characteristic motions forms a group. Each geometry could be associated with a group of motions; for example, in Euclidean geometry the set of motions that defines the geometry is the set of all rotations and translations that can be applied to any figure. (In a *translation* the figure is

If this sounds too abstract to be useful, notice that the set of positive rational numbers under the operation of multiplication is a group: (1) If we multiply any two positive rational numbers together the result is another positive rational number; (2) multiplication is associative; (3) the identity is the number 1; and (4) the inverse of any positive rational number a is just $1/a$.

Once mathematicians had formulated the definition of group, they found groups everywhere. Furthermore breakthroughs in understanding the abstract mathematical properties of groups gave insight into the more "practical" expressions of groups. Some of the first applications of group theory remain some of the best known. Early in the 19th century the theory of groups was used to solve the most intractable problems in mathematics up to that time. For centuries mathematicians had sought to find a formula analogous to the quadratic formula that would enable them to solve certain classes of algebraic equations. By use of the theory of groups it was shown that the formulas they sought did not exist. This discovery demonstrated the power of group theory, but it was only the beginning. Today group theory is used in theoretical computer science, physics, and chemistry as scientists seek to find and exploit structure in information theory, atomic physics, and materials science. Group theory is also used in many branches of mathematics as a tool. It constitutes a separate discipline within the field of algebra.

moved along a straight line without rotation.) These are called Euclidean motions. The geometric properties of Euclidean geometry—lengths and angular measurements—are exactly those properties that remain unchanged under every Euclidean motion. Furthermore two such motions can be combined to yield a third motion by first performing one motion on a figure—a translation, for example—and then performing the second motion—either a translation or rotation—on the same figure. We call this combination of two motions the product of the motions. The set of all such motions, when combined in this way, forms a group called the group of Euclidean motions. Once this was done, Klein dropped the interpretation of the group as a set of motions and looked only at the detailed structure of that group itself.

Aided by von Staudt's reformulation of the ideas of projective geometry, Klein discovered that the set of all projective motions also forms a group. The elements in this group of motions leave other properties—for example, the cross-ratio or the property of being a conic—unchanged. (Geometers usually call projective "motions" by another name, projective transformations, but the idea is the same.) Klein discovered that compared with the group of Euclidean motions, the group of all projective motions has a somewhat more complicated structure.

These observations enabled him to compare projective geometry and Euclidean geometry in terms of their groups of motions. This description revealed how Euclidean and projective geometry are related to each other. But Klein went further. He managed to categorize every geometry that had been discovered by its group of motions. In concept the idea is similar to what biologists do when they compare species of animals. They look for similarities and differences in structure and function and use this information to create a taxonomy. The taxonomy shows how the different species are related. Of course, to do this they have to compare skeletal structures and other characteristics that are not immediately visible to the eye. In a mathematical way Klein did the same thing. First he described the group of motions associated with each geometry; then he used this information to compare one group with another. The comparison showed how the different geometries are related to each other. In general Klein's investigations, called the Erlangen Programme after the university where he had begun work on the project, restored order to the field of geometry. His observations continue to be an important part of geometry today.

Klein's comparison of Euclidean and projective geometry revealed a surprising relationship between the two. He discovered that to every Euclidean motion there corresponds a projective motion of the same type, but there are many projective motions that are not Euclidean motions. This discovery proved that projective geometry is more fundamental than Euclidean geometry. It proved that Euclidean geometry is actually a very special case in the larger and more inclusive field of projective geometry.

7

A NON-EUCLIDEAN
GEOMETRY

The 19th century saw the birth of so-called non-Euclidean geometries. Projective geometry, although it is a branch of geometry quite distinct from Euclidean geometry, still seems intuitive because it can be interpreted as the problem of representing three-dimensional images on a two-dimensional surface. Projective ideas still seem familiar to the modern reader. Some non-Euclidean geometries, however, violate our commonsense notions of space. In this section we describe the first of the nonintuitive, non-Euclidean geometries. The pictures that are associated with this geometry strike many people as strange even today. At the time it was first proposed, many people considered this geometry ridiculous. As a consequence the creator of the new geometry was largely ignored and occasionally ridiculed for his work. The person who was first scorned and later celebrated for making a radical break with the past was the Russian mathematician Nikolai Ivanovich Lobachevsky (1792–1856), sometimes called "the Copernicus of geometry." It was he, more than any other, who worked to show that geometries that are radically different from Euclid's are possible.

Lobachevsky was one of three children in a poor family. His father died when Nikolai was seven years old. Despite the difficulties involved Nikolai eventually enrolled in Kazan University, where he studied mathematics and physics. He remained at Kazan University as a teacher and administrator for most of his life. As a teacher he taught numerous and diverse courses in mathematics and physics. As an administrator he held many positions within the university, and throughout his career he worked hard to make it a better institution. He worked at a furious pace. A strong education had rescued Lobachevsky from a difficult life. He clearly believed that education is the way forward for others as well, and he strove to ensure that a good education awaited those who chose the University of Kazan. In many ways the university was as central to Lobachevsky's life as was his mathematics.

Nikolai Ivanovich Lobachevsky. His far-reaching insights into the nature of geometric truth attracted little attention during his life. (Library of Congress, Prints and Photographs Division)

Lobachevsky was fascinated with Euclid's fifth postulate. The fifth postulate, sometimes called the parallel postulate, was described in detail in the third chapter of this book. It states,

> If a transversal (line) falls on two lines in such a way that the interior angles on one side of the transversal are less than two right angles, then the lines meet on that side on which the angles are less than two right angles.
>
> *(Euclid of Alexandria.* Elements. *Translated by Sir Thomas L. Heath* Great Books of the Western World. *Vol. 11. Encyclopaedia Britannica, 1952.)*

See the illustration on page 30. The fascination with the fifth postulate stems from the fact that it seems so obvious. To many mathematicians it seemed as if it should be possible to *prove* that the two lines that are the subject of the fifth postulate intersect and that they must intersect on the side that Euclid indicates. It was as apparent to them—as it is apparent to most of us—that when two lines *appear* as if they will intersect, it should be possible to *show* that they will, in fact, intersect. For a long time it seemed unnecessary to require a separate postulate to state that the two lines in question will, in fact, intersect. The goal then became to prove that the lines will intersect by using all of Euclid's axioms and postulates except the fifth postulate. For two millennia mathematicians attempted to prove the fifth postulate. As a result of their efforts the fifth postulate became as famous as the three classical unsolved problems in Greek geometry, the trisection of the angle, the squaring of the circle, and the doubling of the cube. It was also as resistant to solution.

By the time that Lobachevsky had begun trying to prove the fifth postulate, mathematicians had already established a 2,000-year record of failure. Many "proofs" that the fifth postulate was a logical consequence of Euclid's other axioms and postulates had been proposed over the years. Each time closer examination, however, showed that each proof had actually assumed that Euclid's fifth postulate was true in order to "prove" it. All of these so-called proofs had to be rejected, because logically speaking they were not proofs at all. One cannot prove a statement is true and simultaneously use the statement in the course of the proof. Toward the end of the 1700s the pattern of attempting to prove the fifth postulate, coupled with the subsequent failure to do so, had become so familiar that some mathematicians had begun to suggest that Euclid had gotten it right after all. They had begun to think that mathematically speaking the fifth postulate was not a logical consequence of anything else in Euclidean geometry but was a stand-alone idea. One could accept it or reject it, but one could not prove it as a consequence of the other postulates, axioms, and definitions that make up Euclidean geometry.

Expressed in this way, the argument about Euclid's fifth postulate strikes most people as reasonable enough. It is the next step, the conceptual step that Lobachevsky had the imagination and boldness to make, that many of us still find difficult to accept. Why is this so? The truth is that although most people do not think much about Euclidean geometry, most of us are nonetheless intellectually and emotionally invested in what Euclidean geometry sometimes purports to represent: the world around us. This is what made Lobachevsky's idea so controversial.

To understand Lobachevsky's idea we rephrase the fifth postulate. This alternate version of the fifth postulate is expressed as follows:

> Given a line, *l*, and a point, *P*, not on *l*, it is possible to construct exactly one line that passes through *P* and is parallel to *l*.

This alternate version of the fifth postulate is logically equivalent to Euclid's version of the fifth postulate in the sense that if we assume Euclid's version then we can *prove* that the alternate version is true. In addition we can prove Euclid's fifth postulate is true *if we begin by assuming* that the alternate version of the fifth postulate is true. Briefly the fifth postulate is true if and only if the alternate version of the fifth postulate is true.

Lobachevsky's great insight was that if the fifth postulate is really a thing apart from the other axioms and postulates of Euclid's geometry, then he should be able to develop a new, logically consistent geometry by simply replacing the fifth postulate by a different postulate. Lobachevsky's alternative to the fifth postulate reads as follows:

> Given a line, *l*, and a point, *P*, not on *l*, there exist at least two straight lines passing through *P* and parallel to *l*.

In other words there are two *distinct* lines, which we have labeled as l_1 and l_2, that pass through the point *P* and are parallel to *l* (see the accompanying diagram; we emphasize that both l_1 and l_2 lie in the plane of the diagram). In Lobachevsky's geometry neither l_1 nor l_2 intersects with *l*, not because they do not extend far enough, but because they are both parallel with *l*. It is also "clear" to most people that line l_2 must eventually intersect line *l* if both are extended far enough, but this belief cannot be proved. Proving

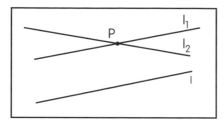

Lobachevsky's alternative to the fifth postulate: Given a line l and a point P not on l, there exist two distinct lines passing through P and parallel to l.

that l_2 will intersect with l is equivalent to proving Euclid's fifth postulate! This was the conceptual barrier that Lobachevsky had to cross, but once he crossed it, he found that he could develop a logically consistent geometry.

Lobachevsky's geometry was the first of the so-called non-Euclidean geometries, because it was developed from a set of axioms and postulates that were different from Euclid's. It violates our perception of the world around us, but violating one's perceptions has nothing to do with mathematics. In Lobachevsky's geometry, for example, the sum of the interior angles of a triangle is always less than 180°, whereas in Euclidean geometry the sum of the interior angles of a triangle is always precisely 180°. We emphasize that Lobachevsky's geometry is not mathematically wrong. It is logically self-consistent, and in mathematics we can ask for nothing more. Admittedly it is not a geometry that appeals to the commonsense notions of most people, but mathematically speaking *it contains no errors.* From the point of view of the mathematician Lobachevsky's geometry is as valid as Euclid's.

It would be easy to dismiss Lobachevsky's insights as clever but meaningless. It is still "obvious" to most of us that in the preceding diagram l_2 intersects with l. It would, however, be a mistake to dismiss Lobachevsky's insights as a mere formalism. Lobachevsky opened up whole new concepts of geometry, which have had important ramifications in both mathematics and science. Since Albert Einstein published his ideas about relativity theory in the early years of the 20th century, many mathematicians and physicists have been busy working out the logical consequences of the theory. To appreciate Lobachevsky's contribution it is important to note that Einstein's ideas made essential use of non-Euclidean geometry. Lobachevsky's keen intellect and willingness to publish ideas that were simply too foreign for most of his contemporaries to appreciate helped make the breakthroughs of the 20th century possible.

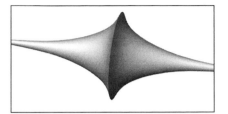

Lobachevsky's geometric ideas can be realized by doing geometry on the surface of this object, called a pseudosphere.

Lobachevsky was not alone in discovering non-Euclidean geometry. Three other people also did. Lobachevsky published first, but he did not influence the others. In each case the discovery of non-Euclidean geometry was made independently. The other name most often associated with the discovery of non-Euclidean geometry is that of the Hungarian mathematician János Bolyai (1802–60). János received his early education in mathematics from his father and later attended the Royal Engineering College in Vienna. His father, Farkas Bolyai, an accomplished mathematician himself, had spent a great deal of effort trying to prove that the fifth postulate is a consequence of Euclid's other axioms and postulates. He warned János, who was then a young military officer, against the study of the fifth postulate, which he thought could only lead to disappointment.

Perhaps the warning had an effect, but not the one that the father had intended. János Bolyai did study the fifth postulate, but he did not spend much time trying to prove it. Instead he replaced the fifth postulate with his own postulate. Bolyai's postulate asserted that given a line and a point not on the line, there exist infinitely many distinct lines through the given point and parallel to the given line. (This assertion is similar, but not identical, to that of Lobachevsky.) Bolyai then researched the geometry that resulted from the substitution of his axiom for Euclid's fifth postulate.

Bolyai's discoveries about non-Euclidean geometry, entitled *Absolute Science of Space*, were published as an appendix to a work of his father's. The father's book had the long and charming title *An Attempt to Introduce Studious Youth to Elements of Pure Mathematics*. As Lobachevsky's work was, Bolyai's work was self-consistent and therefore mathematically correct. As Lobachevsky's work was, Bolyai's *Absolute Science of Space* was also a major break with past geometric thinking. It was published a few years after Lobachevsky first published his own thoughts, but Bolyai developed his ideas contemporaneously with Lobachevsky.

The importance of János Bolyai's discovery of non-Euclidean geometry, as of Lobachevsky's, was not recognized in his lifetime. It is worth noting that both Farkas and János Bolyai were "Renaissance men." The father was a poet, playwright, and musician in addition to being a mathematician. The son, in addition to being an accomplished mathematician, was a violin prodigy and a renowned swordsman.

IS OUR WORLD EUCLIDEAN?

Carl Friedrich Gauss (1777–1855) knew that one consequence of the non-Euclidean geometry described by Lobachevsky is that the sum of the interior angles of a triangle is always *less* than 180°. (In Euclidean geometry the sum of the interior angles of a triangle is always precisely 180°.) Moreover in Lobachevsky's geometry one can also prove that the sum of the measures of the interior angles of a triangle diminishes as the area of the triangle increases. These contrasting theorems about the angles of triangles offered Gauss the opportunity to compare the world around us with the theorems of Euclidean geometry and with the theorems of Lobachevsky's non-Euclidean geometry. To compare the real world with the results of the two geometries, he needed only to measure the angles of real triangles and see whether or not the sum of the angles differs from 180°. Through the use of precise measurements it is, in theory, possible to determine which geometry more accurately represents the conditions around us. Accurate measurements of the interior angles of triangles, thought Gauss, might enable him to determine whether the world is not Euclidean.

This type of approach, however, is not guaranteed to succeed. The difficulty, as Gauss well knew, arises because he planned to use measurements to check mathematical results. Mathematics is an exact science. Measurements are necessarily inexact. In mathematics when we assert that the sum of the interior angles of a triangle is 180°, we assert something that can never be proved by measurement. No matter how precisely we measure there is always some margin of error in our measurements.

The other two names associated with the development of non-Euclidean geometry are those of the German mathematician and physicist Carl Friedrich Gauss (1777–1855) and the much less well-known Ferdinand Karl Schweikart. Gauss was one of the outstanding mathematicians and physicists of the 19th century. Although he entered university to study languages, he soon became interested in mathematics. His Ph.D. dissertation contained the proof of what is now called the fundamental theorem of algebra, which, as the name implies, is a very important insight into the field of algebra. Gauss eventually found work at the University of Göttingen. He remained at the university throughout his working life as both a

Although Gauss's measurements could not possibly verify that the sum of the interior angles of a triangle is precisely equal to 180°, he might nevertheless be able to verify that the sum of the angles is different from 180°. He would be successful in this regard if his margin of error were smaller than the difference between 180° and the number he obtained from the measurements he made of the angles of a triangle. If he could show that the sum of the measures of the interior angles of a triangle was *not* 180°, then he would have proved that Euclidean geometry is *not* a completely accurate description of the world around us. If, however, all he could show was that within the limits of precision of his measurements, the sum of the interior angles of a triangle might be 180° then he would have proved nothing. Gauss set out to search for a negative result.

Fortunately Gauss had the opportunity to supervise a very-large-scale surveying project. As part of the work he had highly accurate devices placed on the summits of three distant mountains—thereby forming a triangle—and he used these devices to make a series of measurements at the triangle's vertices, which were located at the tops of the three summits. Recall that one theorem of the non-Euclidean geometry with which Gauss was familiar was this: The larger the area of the triangle, the smaller is the sum of the interior angles. Therefore the larger the triangle one measures, the easier it should be to note any discrepancies between the actual sum and the 180° of Euclidean geometry. This was the reason he used widely separated mountain summits as the vertices of his triangle. Within the limitations of the accuracy of the measurements Gauss obtained, however, he was not able to disprove the Euclidean assertion that the sum of the angles equals 180°.

professor of mathematics and head of the university's observatory. Among his many interests Gauss also took time to think about Euclid's fifth postulate and he, too, considered the possibility of developing a geometry using a different set of axioms and postulates from those found in Euclid's *Elements*. Gauss, however, feared controversy, and he was aware that publishing the results of a non-Euclidean geometry might produce more heat than light. He kept his thoughts largely to himself and did not publish on the subject. He did, however, correspond with a professor of law named Ferdinand Karl Schweikart (1780–1859), who had developed the same ideas. Little is known about Schweikart, but whatever his reasons, he, too, did not publish his ideas.

These early ideas about non-Euclidean geometries were proposed before most people, even most mathematicians, were prepared to accept them. Eventually, however, these new concepts prepared the way for a fresh look at geometry. As scientists and mathematicians became accustomed to the idea that other geometries exist in a mathematical sense, they discovered, much to their surprise, that other geometries exist in nature as well. Some of the new geometries proved to have physical as well as mathematical meaning.

PART THREE

COORDINATE GEOMETRY

8

THE BEGINNINGS OF ANALYTIC GEOMETRY

There have been very few equations in the first two-thirds of this book, because these geometries were developed largely without algebraic symbolism. Although one does not need algebra to study geometry, algebra can be a great help. The concepts and techniques used in the study of algebra sometimes make difficult geometry problems easy. The discovery of analytic geometry, the branch of geometry whose problems and solutions are expressed algebraically, accelerated the pace of mathematical and scientific progress, because it allowed scientists and mathematicians the opportunity to use insights from both geometry and algebra to understand both better.

Beginning in the Renaissance European algebra became progressively more abstract. Especially important was the increasing use of specialized algebraic notation. When the French mathematician and lawyer François Viète (1540–1603) first used letters to represent classes of objects in a way that is similar to the way we first learn to "let x represent the unknown," he attained a new level of abstraction. Today this is a familiar and often underappreciated algebraic technique, but its importance is difficult to overstate. By using letters to represent types of objects Viète had discovered a new kind of language that could be used to represent all sorts of logical relationships. In particular Viète had found a language that could be used to study the relationships among points, curves, volumes, and other geometrical objects. It had the potential to change mathematicians' concept of geometry.

To merge the disciplines of algebra and geometry, however, mathematicians needed to identify a conceptual "bridge" between these two isolated disciplines. Coordinates acted as the bridge between algebra and geometry. Coordinates enabled mathematicians to perceive geometric spaces as sets of numbers that could be manipulated algebraically. What, then, are coordinates?

Coordinates are ordered sets of numbers. The word *ordered* serves to emphasize the fact that the coordinates (1, 3) are not the same as (3, 1). A coordinate system enables the user to establish a correspondence between sets of numbers and points in space. This must be done in such a way that every point in space can be identified by a set of coordinates and every suitable set of coordinates identifies a unique point in space.

The simplest example of this phenomenon is the so-called real numberline, a line whose points have been placed in one-to-one correspondence with the set of real numbers. To construct this correspondence we choose a point on the line and call that point 0. The points to the left of 0 are placed to correspond to the negative numbers. The points to the right of 0 are placed to correspond to the set of positive numbers. Next we choose one more point to the right of 0 and call that point 1. The distance from 0 to 1 gives a scale to our line. The correspondence is now fixed. The point that will be placed in correspondence with 2, for example, is located to the right of 0 and is twice as far from 0 as is the number 1. In fact given any number we can now identify the point with which it is paired; conversely, given any point on the real line, we can identify the number with which it is paired. In this case we say that the correspondence between the real numbers and the points on the real line is one-to-one: For each point there is a unique number, and for each number there is a unique point.

Longitude and latitude form a system of coordinates that enables the user to identify any position on Earth. This is an example of a correspondence between coordinates—in this case the coordinates are ordered pairs of numbers—and points on the surface of a sphere. Traditionally the first coordinate is the longitude. The longitude identifies how many degrees east or west the location of interest is from the prime meridian. (The prime meridian is chosen

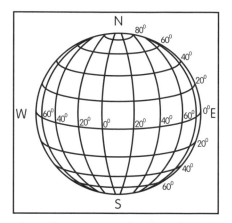

A coordinate system for identifying the position of points on a sphere

so that it is 0°. The longitude tells the user that the location is on a specific line connecting the North Pole with the South Pole. Knowing the longitude is, by itself, not enough to identify a position on the globe. It provides no information about where on that line the location of interest might be found. This is the function of the second coordinate, the latitude. The latitude identifies how many degrees north or south of the equator the point is located. The point is located where the line of longitude and the line of latitude cross. (Notice that there are two exceptional points in this scheme, the North Pole and the South Pole. There is only one point on Earth that is 90° north of the equator, the North Pole. There is no need to give the latitude. A similar statement holds for the South Pole.)

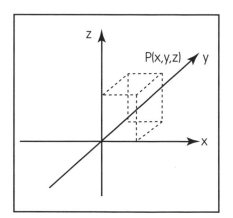

A coordinate system for identifying the position of points in three-dimensional space

This scheme can be carried out for any sphere. We begin by identifying the "north pole." The north pole can be chosen arbitrarily. Once we have identified the north pole, the position of the south pole is also determined. Imagine a straight line entering the sphere at the north pole and passing through the center of the sphere. The point on the surface where the line exits the sphere is the south pole. The equator is the set of all points on the sphere that are equidistant from the two poles. This set of points forms a circle. Choose a single point on this circle, and call this point 0. The line of longitude that connects the north pole with the south pole and passes through 0 is the prime meridian. This completes the scheme. Now every point on the sphere can be identified with two numbers, the longitude, which identifies how many degrees east or west of the prime meridian the point is located, and the latitude, which identifies how many degrees north or south of the equator the point is located.

Another example of a coordinate system is the system used for identifying points in three-dimensional space. Choose a single point (called the origin). Draw three mutually perpendicular real lines through the origin. Call one line the x-axis, the second line the y-axis, and the third line the z-axis. Each line is a copy of the real number line already described. Each point in space can now be uniquely identified with three "coordinates" (see the accompanying diagram). The coordinates must always be listed in the same way: As a rule the first coordinate is the x-coordinate; the second is the y-coordinate; and the last is the z-coordinate. As a consequence the point identified by the three numbers (1, 2, 3) is different from the point (3, 2, 1).

Besides those described here, many other, very different coordinate systems have been developed over the years as mathematicians and scientists have sought to describe various spaces in ways that are convenient and useful.

Menaechmus and Apollonius of Perga

Menaechmus (ca. 380 B.C.E.–ca. 320 B.C.E.) was a prominent Greek mathematician of his time. Unfortunately none of his works has survived. It is solely through the writings of other Greek philosophers and mathematicians that we know of Menaechmus at all. Worse, little about his life or his contributions to mathematics is known for certain. He is described as a student of Eudoxus. It is known that he studied conic sections, and some scholars claim that it was he who coined the terms *parabola*, *hyperbola*, and *ellipse*. He also seems to have been very close to discovering a way to express geometric relationships through a system of coordinates.

Menaechmus is most closely associated with the problem of finding *mean proportionals*. Algebraically the problem is easy to express: Given two numbers, which we represent with the letters a and b, find two unknown numbers—we call them x and y—such that $a/x = x/y$ and $x/y = y/b$. (This statement is simple only because it is expressed in modern algebraic notation. Menaechmus's description was almost certainly more complicated.) From the first of these two equations we can conclude that $ay = x^2$; this is a standard algebraic description of a parabola. The second equation tells us that we can substitute y/b in the first equation for x/y. If we do this, and we cross-multiply, we obtain $ab = xy$; this is an equation for a hyperbola (again in modern notation). This problem seems to indicate that Menaechmus was, in some general way, looking at relationships between variables. Because Menaechmus had no algebra, he was expressing these ideas in terms of line segments and surfaces and curves, but it is not much of a jump from his description of the problem to our more modern coordinate description of the same problem.

Menaechmus is sometimes credited as the first of the ancient mathematicians to use coordinates. Because we are so accustomed to using coordinates to identify everything from positions on game boards to positions in space, it certainly seems as if Menaechmus was close to doing that. But the Greeks had no algebra at that time. The conceptual jump that is so easy for us to make was probably beyond what Menaechmus perceived in his own method.

Another figure who was close to a modern conception of coordinates was Apollonius of Perga. Apollonius was one of the major figures in the history of ancient Greek mathematics. His biography and his contributions have already been described elsewhere in this volume. He is unique among ancient mathematicians because he did invent a coordinate system.

Apollonius was a prolific mathematician, but many of his works did not survive to our own time. Most of his works are known only because they are mentioned in the writings of other mathematicians. The one major work of Apollonius that has survived to modern times largely intact is *Conics*, a book about the mathematical properties of parabolas, hyperbolas, and ellipses, the so-called conic sections. It is in *Conics* that we find the first systematic use of a coordinate system.

Apollonius's understanding and use of coordinates are very different from what we are familiar with today. Today we generally begin with a coordinate system. We imagine a pair of lines, the coordinate axes, and on these lines we graph the curve in which we have an interest. This is something that Apollonius never did. He began by describing a conic section, and then, as an aid to solving certain problems relating to the conic section of interest, he constructed a coordinate system using the conic itself. One of Apollonius's coordinate axes was a line that was tangent to the conic. The other axis was the diameter of the conic. (The *diameter* of the conic is an axis of symmetry.) This method results in a skewed system of coordinates in the sense that the resulting axes are not perpendicular to one another. This is another big difference between the coordinate systems in general use today and Apollonius's system. Today our coordinate axes are generally chosen to be perpendicular to one another. The reason is practical: Perpendicular axes facilitate certain kinds of computations. There is, however, no theoretical need for coordinate axes to be perpendicular. Even when the coordinate axes are skewed, each point on the plane can be identified by a unique set of coordinates relative to the skewed axes. Moreover the computations that are facilitated by perpendicular axes are still possible with skewed ones; they are, however, more awkward.

The coordinate system pioneered by Apollonius apparently had little influence on his contemporaries. Even Apollonius found only limited use for this idea. It is true that his coordinate system enabled him to organize mathematical space in a new way, and he could even point to problems that he had solved with this new idea. For the most part, however, applications just did not exist. Remember that the Greeks knew only about a dozen curves. One of the reasons that coordinate geometry is useful today is that it offers a very general way of describing many different curves.

With so few curves in their mathematical vocabulary, Greek geometers in general, and Apollonius in particular, had no reason to develop a very general approach to their study of curves. Apollonius's coordinate system was one idea that was, for the most part, far ahead of its time.

René Descartes

The French philosopher, scientist, and mathematician René Descartes (1596–1650) is generally given credit for inventing analytic geometry, the branch of geometry that is studied with algebraic methods. The most common coordinate system in use today, the Cartesian coordinate system, is named in honor of him. Descartes's approach to mathematics was new and important, but it was only a small part of the contribution that he made to Western thought.

René Descartes was born into a life of comfort. Both his parents were members of well-off families. His mother, however, died when Descartes was still an infant. His father was a lawyer. Descartes's father described him as an extremely curious boy who was full of questions. His father enrolled Descartes in the best school available, the Royal College, where Descartes demonstrated unusual proficiency in languages. He was especially gifted at writing in French and Latin, and he demonstrated special interest in mathematics and science. His teachers spoke highly of him, but by Descartes's own account he left the Royal College confused and disappointed because he felt that he knew nothing of which he could be certain. The search for certainty was an important theme in Descartes's thinking.

It was expected that as the son of a lawyer Descartes would himself become a lawyer. This was the path taken, for example, by Descartes's brother. After leaving the Royal College, Descartes attended the University of Poitiers and earned a degree in law, but it was not a vocation in which he had any interest. His indifference to law seems to have caused some friction between him and his father, but Descartes was undeterred. After obtaining his law degree he decided to travel in search of what we might call "life experiences." This search was to take up about 10 years of his life.

Descartes's first adventure consisted of joining the Dutch army as an officer under the leadership of Maurice of Nassau. The Dutch were fighting a war of independence against the Spanish. He did not remain in the army long—perhaps a year—and then resigned. Descartes moved from place to place. He joined and resigned from other armies engaged in other wars, but it is doubtful that he participated in much fighting himself. He was famous for "sleeping in." He also spent time seeking the company of interesting people. One newfound friend, the Dutch philosopher and mathematician Isaac Beeckman, introduced him to the algebra of François Viète, a subject that had not been taught to Descartes in school.

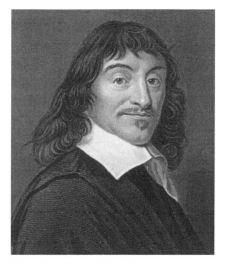

René Descartes. His ideas about the relationships between algebra and geometry influenced the development of both fields. (Topham/The Image Works)

During his travels Descartes lived in Germany, Holland, Hungary, and France. He met and became friendly with Father Marin Mersenne, who gave freely of his time to promote science throughout Europe. Descartes began to be recognized as an insightful and innovative thinker. At last he decided to settle down and begin writing about what he had learned. He moved to Holland, and though he frequently changed residences, he remained in Holland for most of the next 20 years.

It was during his stay in Holland that Descartes produced almost all of the work for which he is known today. He studied philosophy, optics, meteorology, anatomy, mathematics, and astronomy. His first goal, however, was to invent a new science that would unite the many disparate, quantitative branches of knowledge that were developing throughout Europe. Facts, he believed, were not enough; he sought a philosophical context into which he could place discoveries. Descartes's goal was to develop a unified theory of everything.

He began to believe that in large measure he had succeeded. In Descartes's view his science, math, and philosophy were completely intertwined. Although Descartes's philosophical ideas continue to be subjected to critical scrutiny, some of his ideas about science were later shown to be false. His work in mathematics, on the other hand, has become part of mainstream mathematical thought. In this volume we emphasize Descartes's contributions to mathematics; Descartes, however, probably perceived his work in a different context.

Descartes's main mathematical work is contained in the book *Discours de la méthode* (Discourse on method). It is in this book that Descartes makes his contribution to the foundations of analytic geometry. Much of the *Discours* is given over to the interplay between geometry and algebra, but not all of it is new. When Descartes rephrased algebra problems in the language of geometry, he was going over old ground. Islamic mathematicians had done the same sort of thing centuries earlier. But because Descartes's notation was so much better than that of the mathematicians who preceded him, he was able to handle more sophisticated problems more easily.

One important conceptual innovation was the way he interpreted algebraic terms: Previous generations of mathematicians had interpreted terms such as x^2 (x squared) as an actual geometric square. They interpreted the concept that we would write as x^3 (x cubed) as a geometric cube. Because ancient Greek mathematicians and the Islamic mathematicians who followed them had insisted on this geometric interpretation for higher powers of x, they were hard pressed to assign a meaning to terms such as x^4, which in this interpretation would be a four-dimensional object. By abandoning this limiting geometric interpretation Descartes changed mathematicians' perceptions of these symbols and made working with them much easier.

Que fi on veut, au contraire, diminuer de trois la raĉine de cete mefme Equation, il faut faire

$$y + 3 \infty x \quad \& \quad yy + 6y + 9 \infty xx,$$

& ainfi des autres. De façon qu'au lieu de

$$x^4 + 4x^3 - 19xx - 106x - 120 \infty 0,$$ 5

on met

$$
\begin{aligned}
y^4 &+ 12y^3 + 54yy + 108y + \ 81 \\
&+ \ 4y^3 + 36yy + 108y + 108 \\
&\qquad\quad\ - 19yy - 114y - 171 \\
&\qquad\qquad\qquad\ - 106y - 318 \qquad\qquad 10 \\
&\qquad\qquad\qquad\qquad\quad - 120
\end{aligned}
$$

$$\overline{y^4 + 16y^3 + 71yy - \ \ 4y - 420 \infty 0.}$$

Qu'en augmentant les vrayes racines, on diminue les fauffes, & au contraire.

Et il eft a remarquer qu'en diminuant les vrayes ra-cines d'vne Equation, on diminue les fauffes de la mefme quantité, ou, au contraire, en diminuant les 15 vrayes, on augmente les fauffes; & que, fi on diminue, foit les vnes, foit les autres, d'vne quantité qui leur foit efgale, elles deuienent nulles, & que, fi c'eft d'vne quantité qui les furpaffe, de vrayes elles de-uienent fauffes, ou de fauffes, vrayes. Comme icy, 20 en augmentant de 3 la vraye racine, qui eftoit 5, on a diminué de 3 chafcune des fauffes, en forte que celle qui eftoit 4 n'eft plus qu'1, & celle qui eftoit 3 eft nulle, & que celle qui eftoit 2 eft deuenue vraye & eft 1, a caufe que — 2 + 3 fait + 1. C'eft pourquoy, en cete 25 Equation,

$$y^3 - 8yy - 1y + 8 \infty 0,$$

il n'y a plus que 3 racines, entre lefquelles il y en a

An excerpt from Discours de la méthode *showing Descartes's algebraic notation* (Courtesy of University of Vermont)

Descartes also sought to rephrase geometry problems in the lan-guage of algebra, an important innovation. This may seem a triv-ial goal, but synthetic geometry, which is geometry that is expressed via diagrams and without algebraic symbols, can be very taxing to read and understand. It is so hard that the complicated diagrams and accompanying descriptions can themselves be a

ALGEBRAIC NOTATION IN GEOMETRY

One of Descartes's goals in establishing the branch of mathematics now called analytic geometry was to dispense with the difficult presentations that were characteristic of the ancient Greek mathematics. To see why this was important to Descartes and the history of mathematics we need only look at the style in which the Greeks expressed their geometric ideas. The following theorem is taken from Apollonius's *Conics:*

> If the vertically opposite surfaces are cut by a plane not through the vertex, the section on each of the two surfaces will be that which is called the hyperbola; and the diameter of the two sections will be the same straight line; and the straight lines, to which the straight lines drawn to the diameter parallel to the straight line in the cone's base are applied in square, are equal; and the transverse side of the figure, that between the vertices of the sections, is common. And let such sections be called opposite.

(Apollonius. Conics. *Translated by Catesby Taliafero.* Great Books of the Western World. *Vol. 11. Chicago: Encyclopaedia Britannica, 1952.)*

Even with the accompanying diagram—which itself is very complicated—reading this statement is very taxing. The proof of the statement, which is about two pages long, is even more difficult.

What Descartes did was to replace complex diagrams and long complicated sentences with algebraic equations. Descartes's mathematical notation is not difficult for a modern reader to follow. It looks almost modern. This is surprising until one remembers that we got our notation from his works. As we do, Descartes used a plus sign (+) for addition, a minus sign (−) for subtraction, and letters toward the end of the alphabet for variables. There are only a few differences between his notation for analytic geometry and ours. In place of our equals sign he used a symbol that resembled a not-quite-closed number 8 lying on its side. As we do, he used exponents for powers higher than 2; he, however, wrote xx where we would write x^2. Given, however, that Descartes died more than 350 years ago, the similarities between his notation and contemporary algebraic notation are striking.

barrier to progress. Descartes's goal in this regard was to find a way to express the same concepts in a more user-friendly way. He succeeded. His method of solution involves imagining that the geometry problem of interest is already solved. He suggests giving names to each of the quantities, known and unknown. The known quantities can be taken directly from the problem; they are represented by numbers. The unknown quantities are represented with letters chosen to indicate that they are the quantities to be determined. He then expresses the problem in the form of an equation and solves it algebraically. This, of course, is just what we do whenever we "let x represent the unknown." *Discours de la méthode* contains some of the first instances of this technique of problem solving.

Although there are many similarities between Descartes's mathematics and modern analytic geometry—not surprising, since many modern ideas have their origins in his work—there are also important differences between the modern conception of analytic geometry and Descartes's ideas.

Descartes's use of coordinates was haphazard. There is little indication of the coordinate system that today bears his name. Instead he often used oblique coordinates. (A coordinate system is oblique when the axes meet at nonright angles.) Oblique coordinates work well for identifying points in space, but they make, for example, calculating distances between points on the plane difficult. Descartes seems not to have noticed. Furthermore he failed to see the value of negative coordinates. Most importantly he did not use one of the most important techniques in analytic geometry, a technique that was made possible only by his own work: graphing. Analytic geometry made it possible to use geometric methods (graphing) to investigate the mathematical properties of functions, which are the "raw material" of algebra. Descartes, however, does not graph a single function in his book.

Probably the most important connection between geometry and algebra that Descartes discovered is an observation often referred to as the fundamental principle of analytic geometry: Every indeterminate equation—recall that an indeterminate equation is an equation that has infinitely many solutions—that is expressed in two unknowns represents a curve. By *represents a curve* we mean that each solution of the equation consists of two numbers, one for each unknown. These two numbers can be imagined as representing coordinates on a plane. The set of all such coordinates defines a *locus*, or set of points. That locus of points forms a curve in two-dimensional space.

This observation is a vital bridge between algebraic and geometric ideas. Moreover it greatly expanded the vocabulary of curves that were then available to mathematicians. To appreciate Descartes's observation, keep in mind that the Greeks knew only a dozen or so curves. This poverty of curves was due in part to the fact that they had no convenient way of discovering curves. With Descartes's observation about the relationship between curves and equations it was easy to generate as many curves as one wished. Of course, simply writing a formula for a curve gives no insight into the properties of the curve, but Descartes's observation at least gives a simple criterion for increasing the collection of curves available to mathematicians for study.

Descartes also discovered another important bridge between algebra and the geometry of solid figures. He recognized that in an indeterminate equation involving three variables the resulting set of solution points forms a surface in three-dimensional space. This observation allowed mathematicians to generate three-dimensional shapes of all sorts. Before Descartes it was difficult to get beyond the class of simple forms that were known to the Greeks. After Descartes it became easy to produce as many shapes as one desired. Again his work greatly increased the collection of objects available for study.

Descartes's ideas represented a turning point in the history of mathematics, less as a result of the problems that he solved than of the approach he adopted. Descartes showed mathematicians a new and very productive way of looking at geometry and algebra. His insights provided the spark for a great burst of creative activity in mathematics. Descartes was not alone, however. As innovative as his ideas were, they were ideas whose time had come. Even as Descartes was making some of his most important mathematical discoveries, those same discoveries were being made elsewhere by the French lawyer and mathematician Pierre de Fermat.

Pierre de Fermat

Little is known with certainty about the early life of Pierre de Fermat (1601–65). It is known that he received a law degree from the University of Orleans and that his entire working life was spent in the legal profession. He was, however, interested in much more than the practice of law. It is his accomplishments outside the legal profession for which he is best remembered today

Fermat had a gift for languages and was fluent in several. He enjoyed classical literature and the study of ancient sciences and mathematics. Impressive as these activities are, there seems little doubt that to Fermat they were just hobbies. Over the course of his entire life Fermat published just one article on mathematics. Instead we know of Fermat's discoveries through two sources: posthumous publications and personal correspondence. Fermat corresponded with many of the finest mathematicians of his day. Some of these letters were saved, and it is often from these letters that we learn of what Fermat was doing.

By Fermat's time ancient Greek texts had become widely available and mathematicians knew the names of many lost works—books that did not survive to modern times. The lost works were known only through references to them in the writings of others. A common mathematical undertaking during Fermat's life was the attempt to "restore" these works. Here restoration means that the new author attempted to re-create the work from references found in other ancient texts. Fermat had learned of the existence of a lost work of Apollonius while reading the works of Pappus of Alexandria. The book was *Plane Loci*. (A *locus* is a collection of points determined by some condition. Plane loci are collections of points lying in a plane. In this case the reference is to curves.)

While reconstructing what Apollonius might have written, Fermat noticed that the presentation could be considerably simplified by applying algebra to geometry through the use of coordinates. This observation was made independently of Descartes, and it marks the second beginning of analytic geometry. From this observation Fermat noticed that an indeterminate equation in two unknowns determines a locus of points on the plane. This was the fundamental principle of analytic geometry again, but Fermat's emphasis was somewhat different from that of Descartes. Unlike Descartes, Fermat did graph equations on his coordinate system in a way that is somewhat analogous to the way students learn to graph today. He soon noticed relationships between particular types of equations and particular curves.

He noticed, for example, that the locus of points determined by any first-degree equation in two variables—an equation that we would write in the form $ax + by = c$—is a straight line. He noticed that second-degree equations could be related to various conic sections, and he recognized that the form of an equation is determined by the coordinate system in use. For example, in one coordinate system the equation describing a particular hyperbola can be written in the form $4x^2 - y^2 = 1$, and in another coordinate system the same hyperbola can be described by the equation $11x^2 + 10\sqrt{3}xy + y^2 = 4$. The fact that the same curve can be represented by two such different-looking equations led Fermat to study how changing coordinates changed the resulting equation. He wanted to know when two different-looking equations represented the same curve. He did all of this independently of Descartes.

As Descartes did, Fermat discovered that an indeterminate equation in three variables represents a surface in three-dimensional space. Though this observation would not be fully explored until many years after Fermat's death, Fermat had already, apparently, anticipated the next big step. In his writings he seems to indicate that he was aware that similar relations hold for even more variables. For example, an indeterminate equation in four variables would represent what we would call a four-dimensional surface. Fermat, however, did not explore this radical idea.

Another famous discovery by Fermat stemmed from his study of the works of the ancient Greek mathematician Diophantus. Diophantus, as many ancient mathematicians were, was interested in identifying Pythagorean triples. These are sets of three natural numbers with the property that when each of them is squared, one of the squares is the sum of the other two. For example, (3, 4, 5) is a well-known Pythagorean triple, because $3^2 + 4^2 = 5^2$. It has been known for thousands of years that there are infinitely many Pythagorean triples. Fermat became interested in generalizing this problem. He began by searching for triples of positive integers that have the property that when each number is cubed the sum of two cubes is equal to the third. Stated in symbols, he was searching for positive whole number solutions to the equation $a^3 + b^3 = c^3$. What he discovered is that there are no such triples. Additional work convinced him that there are *no* triples of positive integers that satisfy the equation $a^n + b^n = c^n$ for any positive whole number n greater than 2. He wrote in the margin of his copy of Diophantus's book that he had discovered a remarkable proof of this fact but that the margin was too narrow to contain it.

This little margin note marked the start of the search for the proof of what is now known as Fermat's last theorem. No copy of Fermat's proof has ever been located and many mathematicians have struggled to prove a result that seemed almost obvious to Fermat. Large rewards have been offered for a proof, but until late in the 20th century, Fermat's last theorem had defied all efforts to establish its truth. A complete proof was finally produced by using mathematical ideas that were completely unknown to Fermat.

When Fermat became aware of Descartes's *Discours de la méthode* he began to correspond with Descartes. They did not write to each other directly; they sent their letters through Father Marin Mersenne in Paris. These letters contain discussions about various aspects of mathematics. Although they occasionally disagreed on some particular aspect of mathematics there is little evidence that either was successful in convincing the other to change his mind.

Fermat produced a great body of work. Together with the French mathematician and philosopher Blaise Pascal, he helped to establish the foundations for the theory of probability. He developed some of the concepts that would later become central to the subject of calculus, and he was very enthusiastic about the study of the theory of numbers, which involves the study of the

THE PYTHAGOREAN THEOREM
AND CARTESIAN COORDINATES

The Pythagorean theorem states that for a right triangle the square of the length of the hypotenuse equals the sum of the squares of the two remaining sides. This is a fact about triangles. It has nothing to do with coordinate systems, and, in fact, the Pythagorean theorem was discovered thousands of years before Cartesian coordinate systems were discovered. Nevertheless the Cartesian coordinate system is ideally suited to make use of the Pythagorean theorem.

Imagine a plane, two-dimensional surface on which we have drawn a Cartesian coordinate system. Choose any point on the plane other than the origin of coordinates. Call the coordinates of this point (a, b). We can use the origin, the coordinate axes, and the point (a, b) to construct a right triangle. Draw a line from the origin to (a, b). This line is the hypotenuse of the triangle. The segment of the x-axis extending from the origin to the point $x = a$ forms the second side of the triangle. The third side is formed by the line segment parallel to the y-axis and terminating on the x-axis and at the point (a, b).

The Pythagorean formula then tells us that the distance from the origin to the point (a, b) is $\sqrt{a^2 + b^2}$. In two-dimensional space this is also known as the distance formula. It can be generalized to give the distance between any two points in the plane: The distance between the points (a_1, b_1) and (a_2, b_2) is $\sqrt{(a_1 - a_2)^2 + (b_1 - b_2)^2}$.

The reason this is especially important is that essentially the same formula works in spaces of other dimensions. Though it is nothing more than the Pythagorean theorem, it is called the distance formula because it provides an easy way to measure the distance between any two points. If (a_1, b_1, c_1) and (a_2, b_2, c_2) are any two points in three-dimensional space, the distance between them is given by the formula $\sqrt{(a_1 - a_2)^2 + (b_1 - b_2)^2 + (c_1 - c_2)^2}$. The same general formula works in spaces of dimensions higher than 3. Descartes seems to have given little thought to such spaces, but Fermat wrote a few words that seem to imply that he knew that one could build a geometry in higher-dimensional space. Later in the history of geometry distance formulas that are generalizations of the Pythagorean theorem would become important in the development of a new type of geometry called differential geometry. Differential geometry would also depend on the analytic description of geometric objects that Descartes and Fermat had pioneered.

properties of the set of integers. He wrote to other mathematicians to convince them to take up the study of these problems, but number theory, during the time of Fermat, was not a fashionable subject, and Fermat had little luck in convincing others to pursue it.

Fermat's works, as those of Descartes did, sparked a new era in mathematical research. This French lawyer, linguist, and mathematical hobbyist remains one of the more influential mathematicians in history.

9

CALCULUS AND ANALYTIC GEOMETRY

The analytic geometry of Descartes and Fermat is an important tool for investigating geometry, but it also provides a language in which the ideas of calculus can be expressed. Calculus provided a new, extremely valuable tool for investigating geometry. The first person to publish his ideas on calculus was the German philosopher, diplomat, scientist, inventor, and mathematician Gottfried Leibniz (1646–1716).

It would be hard to overstate how versatile Gottfried Leibniz was or how hard he worked. Leibniz was born into comfortable surroundings. His father, a university professor, died when his son was six years old. Although Leibniz's mother made sure that her son received a good education, Leibniz acquired most of his early knowledge in the family library. From his mother, a very religious woman, Leibniz acquired his interest in religion. Religion would always be an important part of Leibniz's philosophical thinking.

Leibniz was educated at the University of Leipzig. He studied philosophy, Latin, Greek, Hebrew, rhetoric, and a little math. As so many of the mathematicians in this history did, he demonstrated a particular aptitude for languages. It was at Leipzig that Leibniz was first exposed to the new sciences of Galileo, Descartes, and others. These ideas made a deep impression on him and he began to consider the problem of integrating the new sciences with the classical thought of ancient Greece. After he received his degree, Leibniz remained at Leipzig to study law, but at age 20, having completed the requirements for a Ph.D., he was refused the degree, apparently because of his age. When the university refused Leibniz his degree, he left and never returned. He was soon awarded a Ph.D. from the University of Altburg.

Leibniz had little interest in academia. He worked as an ambassador and government official his entire life. Some scholars claim that Leibniz avoided academic life because he could not tolerate the segmentation of knowledge that characterizes the structure of universities. Leibniz was always interested in unifying disparate ideas. Though he made significant contributions to the intellectual life of Europe, he never specialized. He moved easily from one branch of knowledge to the next in pursuit of his intellectual goals—and his goals were extremely ambitious.

Leibniz had been born into a region of Europe that was devastated by the Thirty Years' War, a terrible conflict that had its roots in religious tensions between various sects of Christianity and in territorial aggression among the European powers. With the destruction of the Thirty Years' War still everywhere apparent, Leibniz worked patiently in a lifelong quest to reunite all of the Christian sects.

Another of Leibniz's goals was to harmonize all branches of knowledge. At this time there were many scientific societies, which were often informal groups organized to study and advance the new sciences. Leibniz worked to try to coordinate research and to organize the resulting discoveries in such a way as to illuminate a greater, more inclusive view of the universe. Though Leibniz is best remembered for his contributions to mathematics, his mathematical discoveries were only part of a much larger scheme.

Despite his very broad education, Leibniz was not, at first, a very well-versed mathematician. His first attempts at mathematics were not especially impressive. He used his diplomatic postings to undertake a comprehensive study of mathematics. In particular he studied mathematics under Christian Huygens, one of the foremost scientists and mathematicians of his time. Just as he educated himself as a boy, Leibniz largely acquired knowledge of mathematics through self-directed independent study.

Leibniz had a gift for inventing good mathematical notation. With respect to calculus he gave a great deal of thought to developing a notation that would convey the ideas and techniques that form the basis of the subject. His exposition of the ideas and techniques that calculus comprises is still learned by students today. The symbols d/dx, $\int f dx$, and several others are all familiar to anyone who has ever taken an introductory calculus course. Most of these symbols are Leibniz's innovations.

To appreciate the importance of Leibniz's exposition of calculus, comparing his mathematical legacy with that of Isaac Newton, the codiscoverer of calculus, is helpful. There was a bitter argument between the mathematicians of Great Britain, who accused Leibniz of plagiarizing Newton's work, and the mathematicians living in continental Europe, who argued that Leibniz had discovered calculus independently. (No one argued that Newton was not first, but because he did not publish his ideas, they had little influence until Leibniz's publications spurred Newton to share his discoveries.) The nationalistic feelings that caused the dispute and were simultaneously heightened by it caused many British mathematicians to adopt the symbolism of Newton rather than that of Leibniz. As a consequence for many years after the deaths of Newton and Leibniz, mathematical progress in Great Britain lagged behind that on the Continent, where Leibniz's superior notation had been adopted.

Leibniz did more than express calculus in a way that facilitated future research. He used it to further his understanding of geometry. Calculus can be an extremely important tool in the study of geometry. It can be used to analyze curves and surfaces in a way that cannot be done without it.

Recall that the fundamental principle of analytic geometry states that a single equation in two variables determines a curve. This principle makes writing equations for any number of curves very easy, but gives no insight into what any curve looks like. Consequently mathematicians acquired a new and huge vocabulary of curves whose shapes were often not apparent. How could they discover the properties of a curve that was described solely in terms of an equation? For example, in order to graph a curve one must answer a number of questions: Over what intervals is the curve decreasing or increasing? At what positions, if any, does the curve attain a maximal or minimal value? These are the kinds of questions that can be answered—and often easily—with the help of calculus.

With calculus many more, perhaps less obvious, geometric questions could be answered as well. Mathematicians could determine at what points the curve was steepest, and they could find the area beneath the curve. These questions can be mathematically interesting; moreover, when the curve represents a physical process these questions also have scientific importance. Calculus enabled Leibniz to use new tools to work on old and new problems. The result was a long period of rapid advancement in the mathematical and physical sciences.

Isaac Newton, the New Geometry, and the Old

The new analytic geometry was too useful to ignore, but the geometry of the ancient Greeks was not immediately supplanted by the new ideas. The works of Euclid, Apollonius, and Archimedes represented more than mathematics to the European mathematicians of this time. Greek ideas about philosophy and aesthetics still were very important, and many mathematicians still used the straightedge and compass whenever they could. Nowhere is this better illustrated than in the works of the British mathematician and physicist Isaac Newton (1643–1727).

Isaac Newton was born in the village of Woolsthorpe, Lincolnshire. This village, which still consists of a few houses built along narrow, winding streets, is too small to be found on most maps today. It is about a mile from the town of Colsterworth, which is big enough to appear on maps. Woolsthorpe is about 150 km (90 miles) north northwest of London.

Newton's childhood was a difficult one. His father died before he was born. His mother remarried and sent Newton to live with his grandmother while she moved to a different town to live with her new husband. They reunited several years later after she again became a widow.

As a boy Newton was known for his mechanical inventiveness. He built kites, clocks, and windmills. He attended school in nearby Grantham, where he learned Latin but apparently little more than basic arithmetic. (Most scholarly works were written in Latin at this time.) Later at Trinity College Newton was introduced to the works of Euclid and Descartes. He probably did not learn of the work of Descartes in his classes, however. The universities of this time were still teaching the classical philosophy of Aristotle. The scientific and mathematical revolution begun by Galileo, Descartes, and others had affected everything except the universities. On his own Newton began to read all of the major modern scientific and mathematical treatises as well as classical Greek geometry. He soon mastered these ideas and began to develop his own theories about light, motion, mathematics, and alchemy.

It is an interesting fact about Newton that he was always very much interested in old, quasi-magical ideas about alchemy, the medieval "science" that held out the promise of turning lead into gold. Most thoughtful scientists had already abandoned this mystical set of procedures and beliefs, but Newton carefully hand-copied page after page of alchemy texts into his personal notebooks. Unlike many scientists of his day Newton always looked as far backward as forward.

Though Newton had already begun developing his great scientific and mathematical ideas while he was a student at Trinity College, he kept to himself, and he graduated with little fanfare. No one, apparently, was aware of the work he had accomplished there. In the year that Newton graduated (1665) Trinity College was closed. It

Isaac Newton. He invented a number of different coordinate systems to express his geometric insights. (Library of Congress, Prints and Photographs Division)

remained closed for two years. England had been disrupted by another outbreak of the bubonic plague. In the absence of effective medical treatment there was little to do but isolate infected areas and wait for the plague to subside. During this time Newton did much of his life's work. When Trinity reopened, Newton returned to earn his master's degree. He then joined the faculty.

Today Newton is best remembered for his work in optics, the theory of motion, the discovery of the law of gravity, and the invention of calculus, but he also had an interest in geometry. His approach to geometry was in many ways representative of the attitudes of the time.

Newton never abandoned straightedge and compass geometry. There was no need to continue to perform the straightedge and compass constructions of the ancient Greeks. A straightedge and compass cannot, in the end, construct more than a straight line and a circle. In the hands of the Greeks they had been enough to make many new and interesting discoveries, but by Newton's time mathematics had moved beyond these implements. Analytic geometry—what Newton called the geometry of the moderns— was both more convenient to use and better suited to calculus, the branch of mathematics on which so much of his scientific analyses depended. Nevertheless Newton persisted in the use of the straightedge and compass whenever possible. Even in his most famous work, *Philosophiae Naturalis Principia Mathematica* (Mathematical principles of natural philosophy), better known today as *Principia*, he used the geometry of Euclid rather than the geometry of Descartes as often as possible. In another of his books, *Arithmetica Universalis* (Universal arithmetic), he even rejected the use of equations in geometry. He believed that equations, which were fundamental to the new analytic geometry, had no place in geometry. Geometry, to Newton, meant synthetic geometry, the geometry of diagrams that Descartes had rejected.

Whatever Newton's beliefs about what was proper in geometry, he used analytic methods whenever it was necessary. In fact he was quite creative about several aspects of geometry. One interesting example of Newton's interest in analytic geometry is his development of several new coordinate systems. He describes eight such

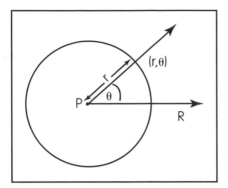

Polar coordinates. The position of point (r, θ) is determined by its distance from P (denoted by r) and the angle formed by the reference ray and the line passing through P and (r, θ)—here denoted by the Greek letter θ, theta.

systems in his book *De Methodus Fluxionum et Serierum Infinitorum* (On the method of series and fluxions—better known as Method of fluxions—is a description of calculus.) One of the coordinate systems, polar coordinates, is widely used today.

In a polar coordinates system each point is identified by a length and an angular measurement. We let the coordinates (*r*, θ) represent this pair; the letter *r* represents the length and the Greek letter θ (theta) represents the angle. To understand Newton's idea imagine a point, *P*, and a ray, *R*, which can be imagined as a very long arrow. The ray *R* has its "tail" located at the point *P*. We make our measurements with reference to *P* and *R*. The length, which is usually represented with the letter *r*, identifies all points that are located a distance *r* from *P*. But the set of all points at a given distance *r* from *P* is a circle centered at *P* of radius *r*. Therefore the length, which is always positive, allows us to identify not a point but a circle. By contrast the angular measurement allows us to identify a second ray. This is the ray with base at *P* that together with *R* forms an angle, θ. The point of interest is located where the ray intersects the circle. To Newton what we call polar coordinates were useful in the study of spirals, although today they are used in a much wider variety of applications (see the accompanying illustration).

Newton had a much broader understanding of Cartesian coordinates than his predecessors had. He was comfortable using negative coordinates. In contrast, Descartes used only positive coordinates. One consequence of the use of negative coordinates is that Newton could consider the entire graph of a function. He could look at the form the function took when the independent variable was negative, so in this sense Newton's graphs are "larger" than those of his predecessors. This very inclusive understanding of Cartesian coordinates enabled him to convey a more complete picture of the properties of functions than his predecessors. Because Newton's functions often represented physical objects or phenomena, he was able to see more clearly into the phenomena that these functions represent.

Newton's numerous coordinate systems are indicative of more than technical skill. They are in part a reflection of the way he sees the universe. Newton sees space as having an absolute quality. He perceives the universe much as we might perceive a stage, as a place where a play unfolds. Strictly speaking the stage is not part of the play; it is the location where the play takes place. Similarly space is, to Newton, a huge, featureless expanse where nature evolves. It is the mute and unchangeable background for everything. Space is the location of the universe, but it is not, strictly speaking, part of the universe. As the stage and the play are, space is, for Newton, the place where the universe unfolds. In Newton's view things happen *in* space; they do not happen *to* space. *Absolute space* is the name often given to this perception of reality.

One consequence of this understanding is that when two observers moving along their own straight-line paths at constant velocities measure the distance between any two objects, they, if neither makes a mistake, arrive at the same measurement. They must arrive at the same measurement because in this model of space they are simply measuring the distance between two fixed points in space. A coordinate system that reflects this type of "sameness" is the three-dimensional Cartesian coordinate system. This model of the universe has proved to be a very useful geometric model, although, as we will see later, it is not the only useful model from which to choose.

Newton has a similar attitude about time. He believes that time is absolute in the same way that he believes that space is absolute. Time, according to Newton, is outside the universe in the same way that a stopwatch is outside a race. A race—a footrace, for

BIPOLAR COORDINATES

Bipolar coordinates, another coordinate system invented by Isaac Newton, show how the choice of coordinates can facilitate the study of planar geometry. Bipolar coordinates are not used very often today, but they make the algebraic description of conic sections extremely easy. To construct a bipolar coordinate system, choose two distinct points. To see how this coordinate system is used, consider two conic sections, an ellipse and a hyperbola.

An ellipse is determined by two points, called foci, and a length. Given two points,

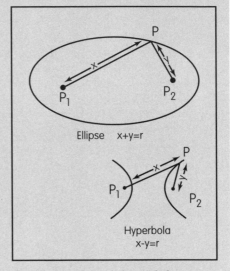

An ellipse, a hyperbola, and their equations expressed in bipolar coordinates.

example—may take place while the stopwatch is running, but the race does not affect the watch, nor the watch the race. In this sense the watch is not part of the race. Similarly the universe unfolds over time, but the processes that occur in the universe do not affect the passage of time. In Newton's view any two observers outfitted with accurate watches measure the same amount of time provided their watches show an equal amount of time has elapsed.

Mathematicians, physicists, and engineers represent these ideas of space and time by using a four-dimensional Cartesian coordinate system. Three of the coordinates are used to identify a point in space, and the fourth coordinate is used to identify a point in time. Positions in this four-dimensional system are often represented with coordinates that look like this: (x_1, x_2, x_3, t), where t represents a point in time and the other coordinates are needed to identify a point in space. Four dimensions are necessary because in which we call P_1 and P_2, and a length, an ellipse is the set of all points, the sum of whose distances from P_1 and P_2 is equal to the given length. To see how this works, let r represent the given length; let P represent a point on the ellipse; and let x and y represent the distances from the point P to P_1 and P_2, respectively. The distances x and y satisfy the equation $x + y = r$. In fact a point is on the ellipse if and only if the distances from that point to P_1 and P_2 satisfy this equation. This equation could not be any simpler looking. By contrast $ax^2 + bx + cy^2 + dx = e$ is the general equation of an ellipse in Cartesian coordinates.

Similarly a hyperbola is determined by two points and a distance. The hyperbola can be defined as the set of all points, the difference in whose distances from the points P_1 and P_2, is a constant r. Therefore the equation of a hyperbola in bipolar coordinates is $x - y = r$ (see the illustration).

In Cartesian coordinates both of the equations $x + y = r$ and $x - y = r$, where x and y are the variables and r is a constant, represent straight lines. The meaning of the equations evidently depends very much on the coordinate system in which they appear. But coordinate systems are mechanisms to convey ideas. The best coordinate system *for a given purpose* is the system that conveys the required information as simply and transparently as possible. Newton was one of the first to understand and employ this principle. Today a variety of coordinate systems are in common use.

order to specify an event of any sort we need to specify its location in space and the time at which it occurs. Newton believes that the same coordinate system can be applied throughout space, because distances and times are the same everywhere for everyone. This model of the geometry of the universe is sometimes called a Newtonian reference frame.

Newton's ideas about the geometry of the universe remained at the heart of Western science for centuries, but they have their limitations. That Newton's geometric perceptions were not (so to speak) universally valid would not be recognized until the 20th century. Newtonian reference frames are still used in most branches of science and engineering, however, because they are accurate enough for most applications. Newton's geometric understanding of space and time is still one of the most used and useful concepts in modern science.

Leonhard Euler and Solid Geometry

The Swiss mathematician Leonhard Euler (1707–83) was a major contributor to the development of analytic geometry. Euler loved mathematics. When he became blind in one eye he is said to have remarked that henceforth he would have less to distract him from his work. This statement turned out to be prophetic. Although mathematics is a highly visual field—equations, graphs, surfaces, and curves are all better seen than heard—Euler had an extraordinary mathematical imagination. He did not depend on his eyes to do mathematics any more than Beethoven depended on his ears to write music.

Euler, for example, was interested in the gravitational interaction of the Sun, Moon, and Earth. These interactions are quite complex, and any realistic mathematical model of this three-body system involves difficult equations with difficult solutions, in part because the geometry of the system changes continually. Euler had attacked the problem with some success when he was middle-aged, but he was not entirely happy with the solution. Many years later he revisited the problem. In the intervening years, however, he had become completely blind. Without vision Euler had to imagine the equations and perform the corresponding computations in his head. His second theory was nevertheless an improvement on the first. In the area of analytic geometry he developed many algebraic techniques and concepts to help him visualize and analyze surfaces in three-dimensional space. The study of the geometric properties of objects in three-dimensional space is called solid analytic geometry.

Euler was not the first person to study solid analytic geometry. Even Descartes had displayed some awareness of ways that surfaces can be described in three dimensions. As discussed earlier in this volume, Descartes observed that a single indeterminate equation in three variables defines a surface in the sense that each solution of the equation is an ordered triplet of numbers and so identifies a point in space. The set of all solutions is a surface whose properties depend on the specific properties of the equation. To use these observations, however, one must go further and establish specific correspondences between particular surfaces and particular equations. Each surface of a certain kind is the solution set for a particular kind of equation. To be sure, Descartes had established an important connection between algebra (the equation) and geometry (the corresponding locus of points), but he lacked the mathematical tools for investigating the properties of surfaces determined in this way. It was left to Euler to begin analyzing the many relationships that exist between equations and surfaces.

To study geometry via algebraic equations Euler had to determine how an equation

Leonhard Euler, one of the most productive mathematicians in history. He greatly extended the frontiers of geometry. (Library of Congress, Prints and Photographs Division)

that describes a surface in one coordinate system changes when the coordinate system itself changes. Changing coordinate systems changes the appearance of the associated equations but only in very specific ways. One of the first problems Euler encountered was establishing when two different-looking equations, each describing a surface in three-dimensional space, actually describe the same surface in different coordinates. He was not the first to address this problem. Fermat had examined the problem earlier, but because mathematics had developed since the time of Fermat, Euler was in a better position to make progress.

Of special interest to Euler in this pursuit were changes to coordinate systems that involve translations—coordinate changes that involve moving the position of the origin of coordinates from one location to another—and rotations—motions that involve rotating the coordinate system about some preassigned axis. Recall that these are the so-called Euclidean transformations: In Euclidean geometry two figures are said to be congruent if one can be made to coincide with the other after a series of translations and rotations. So Euler sought an analytic expression of Euclid's idea of congruence applied to three-dimensional space. This is important: Given two equations, how can one determine whether there exists a change of coordinates consisting of translations and rotations of the coordinate axes that will cause the surface defined by one of the equations to coincide with the surface defined by the other? The answer to this question is often not immediately obvious, and yet if one cannot determine when two objects are the same (or different!), there is not much one can do. One of Euler's principal

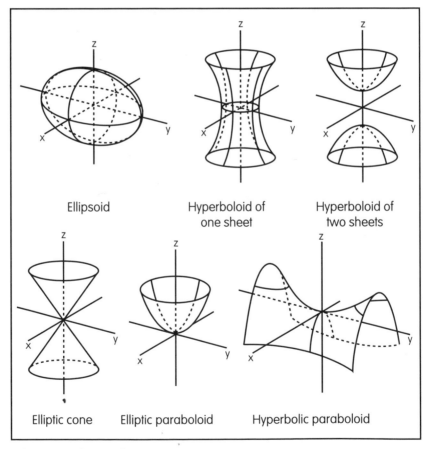

The six quadric surfaces

problems was developing an analytic criterion that would enable him to answer these types of questions.

Not only did Euler search for a generalized analytic expression of congruence, he also generalized the idea of a conic. The generalization he obtained is called a quadric surface. There are six main types of quadric surfaces: the elliptic paraboloid, the hyperbolic paraboloid, the elliptic cone, the ellipsoid, and the hyperboloids of one and two sheets. Each is determined by a second-degree equation in three variables. The surfaces determined by these equations are best compared by changing coordinate systems until each equation is in a standard form. Graphing the surfaces is then relatively easy. The graphs can be compared for similarities and differences. The quadric surfaces were only part of what Euler studied. He also studied other surfaces and attempted a classification of these surfaces that depended on the properties of the equations that defined them.

Euler's work in solid analytic geometry was in one sense groundbreaking. He went much further in the analytic description of three-dimensional objects than anyone had. On the other hand, he seems to have drawn his inspiration from the work done by the ancient Greeks. There is no calculus in what has been described here. Euler's ideas of congruence and the conic sections are almost classical except for the language in which they are expressed. This is part of what makes his ideas so mathematically appealing. They encapsulate Greek geometry, but only as a special case. His ideas on solid analytic geometry are rooted far in the past, but they extend the ancient results into something both new and useful.

Much of Euler's success in the field of analytic geometry resulted from his concept of a mathematical function. Although Descartes, Fermat, Newton, and Leibniz had grappled with the idea of a mathematical function, Euler was the first to use the concept systematically. For Euler functions are often representations of objects—they often represent geometrical objects—to which Euler could apply all of the ideas and techniques that he had done so much to develop. The concept of function is something to which all modern students are exposed early in their education. The modern emphasis on functions, almost to the exclusion of any other approach to mathematics, means that many of us identify functions with mathematics. One can do math without functions, however. There is, for example, no concept of a function in Apollonius's treatment of ellipses, hyperbolas, and parabolas. Functions are not necessary, but they are extremely helpful. By changing the emphasis from synthetic descriptions of curves and surfaces to an algebraic emphasis on functions, Euler was able to move toward a more abstract and ultimately more productive kind of mathematics.

A good example of Euler's use of functions is his parametric representation of surfaces. Systematically parameterizing surfaces was another Euler innovation. He discovered that sometimes it is convenient—even informative—to introduce one or more auxiliary variables into a problem, and then to write curves and surfaces in terms of these auxiliary variables or parameters.

To convey Euler's idea, we begin in two rather than three dimensions and consider the problem of parameterizing a curve. Suppose, for purposes of illustration, that we have a long, thin, straight, flexible wire, and suppose that we draw a curve on a piece of graph paper such that the curve does not cross itself. We can then bend the wire until it follows the curve that has been drawn on the paper. In doing so, we deform the wire into a new shape— mathematicians call this *mapping* the wire onto the curve—but we do not cut or otherwise destroy the wire. By deforming the wire in this way we establish a one-to-one correspondence or "pairing" between the points on the one-dimensional wire and the points on the curve, which exists in a two-dimensional space.

We can identify each point on the wire with a single number, the distance from the given point to one (fixed) end of the wire. Let the letter t represent distance along the wire. Each point on the plane, however, requires two numbers—one ordered pair— to denote its location. Let (x, y) denote a point on the curve. By placing the wire over the curve we establish a one-to-one correspondence between t, the point on the wire whose distance from the beginning of the wire is t units, and (x, y) the points on the curve. This enables us to describe the curve in terms of the functions determined by this correspondence—call the functions $x(t)$ and $y(t)$. The functions $x(t)$ and $y(t)$ are called a parametric representation of the curve.

This is the physical analogy to what Euler did when he parameterized curves. The analog to the straight, thin, flexible wire is the real number line or some segment of it. In place of physically bending the wire, Euler used mathematical functions to describe the distorted shape of the line or line segment. Introducing a parameter in this way enables the mathematician to describe a wide variety of curves more easily. Furthermore parameters are often chosen to represent some physical quantity, such as time or—as in our example—distance. This, of course, is exactly what we do when we describe a distant location (relative to our own location) in terms of the time required to drive there or in terms of the distance along some highway. In that sense parameterizations are not simply convenient: They are also a more natural way of describing curves.

One example of the type of curve to which Euler applied these insights is called a cycloid. A cycloid has an easy-to-imagine mechanical description. It is the path traced out by a particle on the rim of a wheel as the wheel rolls along smooth ground without slipping. If we imagine the wheel rolling along the x-axis in the positive direction, we can use equations involving the trigonometric functions sine and cosine to represent the path of the particle:

$$x = rt - r \sin t$$
$$y = r - r \cos t$$

where t is the parameter and r represents the radius of the wheel. The equations show how the coordinates x and y can be written as functions of the single variable t.

The analogous problem in three dimensions is the parametric representation of surfaces. The physical analogy here is to imagine a flat, thin, flexible sheet of rubber. Suppose that we imagine drawing a Cartesian coordinate system on this flat sheet. If we now imagine a three-dimensional body, we can "capture" or model the shape of the body by stretching our flat sheet of rubber over the body until it fits snugly. In this case we have " mapped" a flat, two-dimensional surface onto a three-dimensional body in such a way that we have again established a one-to-one correspondence. This time

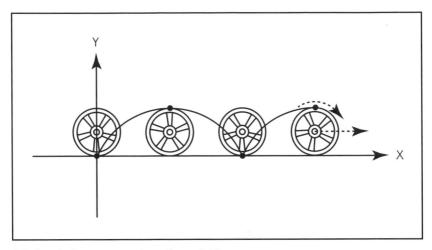

Mechanical representation of a cycloid

the correspondence is between the points on the plane—here represented by the flat sheet of rubber—and the surface of the body. Because the flat sheet is a two-dimensional object, only two numbers are needed to identify any point on the sheet: the x-coordinate and the y-coordinate. On the other hand, every point in three-dimensional space requires three coordinates to identify its position (length, width, height). Consequently if we let the ordered triplet (u, v, w) represent a point in three-dimensional space, and we let (x, y) represent a point in two-dimensional space, parametric equations for a surface are of the form

$$u = u\,(x, y)$$
$$v = v\,(x, y)$$
$$w = w\,(x, y)$$

where we have written the three-dimensional, surface coordinates u, v, and w as functions of the two-dimensional, "sheet" variables x and y.

We can find approximate values for the functions $u(x, y)$, $v(x, y)$, $w(x, y)$ for any ordered pair (x, y) by measuring the position of (x, y) in the three-dimensional coordinate system that we have chosen. The *u*-coordinate of the point, which is called $u(x, y)$, is simply the "length" measurement of (x, y) when measured in our coordinate system. We denote this measurement as $u(x, y)$. The *v*-coordinate is the "width" measurement of (x, y) in the three-dimensional coordinate system—this measurement is $v(x, y)$—and the *w*-coordinate is our measurement of the height of the point (x, y) in our coordinate system, and we denote this as $w(x, y)$.

A simple example of a parametric description of a surface is the following description of a hemisphere, which is described by the equations

$$u(x, y) = x$$
$$v(x, y) = y$$
$$w(x, y) = \sqrt{1 - x^2 - y^2}$$

where the parameters *x* and *y* are restricted to the disk of radius 1, centered at the origin of coordinates.

Having established the existence and general shape of several types of objects, Euler then began to analyze other, more subtle properties; here is where his knowledge of calculus came into play. One important line of inquiry was related to the problem of moving along a curved surface in three-dimensional space: If one is required to stay on the surface, and one is given two points on the surface, what is the shortest path between these two points? The difficulty in finding and computing paths of minimal length is that the old Euclidean maxim "The shortest distance between two points is a straight line" no longer applies. On the curved surface there may not be any "straight" lines to connect the two points. So the problem of determining the shortest distance between two given points can be fairly complicated. The shortest path connecting two given points on a surface is called a geodesic.

Euler opened a new mathematical world with this type of analysis. He was able to describe new types of objects in three-dimensional space and to examine their geometric properties with the new mathematics. This was a huge step forward, and it was immediately recognized as a highly innovative approach. Other mathematicians quickly stepped up to continue the analysis.

GASPARD MONGE

Some of the contributions of Gaspard Monge (1746–1818), as well as a brief biography, have already been described in the section on projective geometry. He deserves mention in the section on analytic geometry as well, because he helped invent it. Monge's interests were very broad. In addition to his work in mathematics, he was a dedicated teacher, a scientist, and a follower of Napoléon. His work for Napoléon, his interests in all matters scientific, and the fact that he taught at several colleges simultaneously diluted his contributions to mathematics. Nevertheless he was such a "natural" geometer that he was able to contribute to several aspects of geometry while pursuing his other obligations and interests.

Monge believed that geometry is the language of mathematics. This was decidedly a minority view at the time. Analysis attracted most of the attention, and with good reason. Euler and others had made extraordinary breakthroughs by using the tools of calculus and related concepts. Progress was rapid and far-reaching. To Monge, however, these developments were not quite satisfying. Monge revisited problems in analysis from the point of view of geometry. He rephrased problems in analysis so that the geometric component of the problem was at the fore. Monge thought geometrically.

To get a feel for the kind of problem of which Monge was particularly fond we briefly review a particular class of problems that he was the first to solve. Imagine two planes in a three-dimensional space. If they are not parallel then they will intersect along the line. (In a Cartesian coordinate system the two planes might be described with the questions $ax + by + cz = d$ and $a'x + b'y + c'z = d'$, where x, y, and z are the variables and a, b, c, d, a', b', c', and d' are numbers called coefficients and are assumed to be known.) Monge used analytic expressions for these planes to obtain an equation for a line. Then he imagined a third plane perpendicular to this line, and he computed the equation of this third plane in terms of the coefficients that were used to describe the first two planes. This problem is the type that Apollonius would surely have enjoyed had he known about analytic geometry. It has the feeling of Greek geometry but it is expressed analytically. Monge, as Euler did, also studied quadric surfaces, the three-dimensional generalizations of the conic sections. His work is a nice synthesis of the aesthetics of Greeks and the mathematics that grew out of the work of Descartes, Newton, and Euler.

Finally, by combining the ideas and observations of Descartes and Fermat with the new analysis, these mathematicians produced an approach to geometry that is still studied and used extensively today. What has changed is the perception of the geometry. When Euler and others sought to describe various surfaces, they were doing work that was perceived by their contemporaries as highly abstract. Today, the same types of problems that Euler and others studied are often associated with research in applied mathematics and engineering. Their old discoveries are used in ways that the discoverers could not have anticipated. This is a nice example of how what is perceived as pure mathematics by one generation of researchers is perceived as applied mathematics by a later generation of researchers.

10

DIFFERENTIAL GEOMETRY

Euler made great strides in developing the necessary conceptual tools for representing and analyzing surfaces and curves. His emphasis, however, was on describing surfaces globally; that is, he sought to describe the surface of an entire object rather than develop a careful analysis of the properties of a surface near a point on the surface. Analyzing a small part of a surface in the neighborhood of a point is called a local analysis. Though, at first glance, a local analysis may seem to be less interesting than a global analysis, time has proved otherwise. The first person to see the value of local analysis was the German mathematician and physicist Carl Friedrich Gauss (1777–1855). He is generally regarded as the founder of the subject of differential geometry, a branch of geometry that uses the tools of analysis, that branch of mathematics to which calculus belongs, to study the local properties of surfaces. (Gauss's contributions to non-Euclidean geometry are recounted earlier in this volume.)

To understand Gauss's work in differential geometry, knowing that he was also interested in the very practical field of geodesy, which involves the determination of the exact size and shape of Earth and the precise location of points on Earth, is useful. In fact, he directed a very large surveying effort for his government. The problem of producing the most accurate possible flat maps of curved surfaces is a good introduction to some ideas of differential geometry.

Many of us take the accuracy of maps for granted. The maps that we use seem to indicate precise locations, sizes, and shapes of geographic features. But all of these maps contain inaccuracies, and the larger the areas that are mapped, the greater the inaccuracies the maps have. Some causes of distortion are obvious: A flat street map of San Francisco, for example, fails to capture the steep hills that are characteristic of that city. This results in a distortion of short distances. Furthermore the angles at which the city streets meet on the map may not correspond to the angles made by the streets themselves. This, too, is the result of representing a curved surface on a flat map. In fact, every map of a state, a county, or even a large city *must* distort distances, even when the terrain is not at all hilly, because no geographical feature of even modest size is flat. Earth itself is round, and the geometric properties of its large geographic areas must reflect the curved surface on which they are situated.

Mathematically one method of approaching mapmaking is through the use of something called a tangent plane. Consider a sphere and a plane. Imagine positioning the plane so that it touches the sphere at exactly one point. The plane is said to be tangent to the sphere at the point of contact. There is only one tangent plane at each point along the surface of the sphere, or, to put it another way, any two planes that are tangent to a sphere at a given point must coincide. One consequence of the uniqueness of the tangent plane is that it is the best flat approximation to the sphere at the point of tangency.

One method of making a good map near the point of tangency involves projecting the region of interest onto the tangent plane. This process is *stereographic projection.* To see how this might be done, imagine placing a sphere on a plane so that the sphere rests on a single point, which we will call the south pole. Now imagine a line passing through the south pole and the center of the sphere.

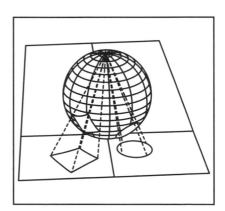

Stereographic projection of figures on a sphere to a plane

Extend this line until it intersects the top of the sphere, and call this point of intersection the north pole. Transferring the lines of latitude and longitude drawn on the sphere onto the plane is, in principle, a simple matter: Extend a line from the north pole through a point of the sphere until it intersects the tangent plane. This procedure establishes a one-to-one correspondence between points on the sphere and points on the plane. Every point on the sphere is mapped to a point on the plane except the north pole. The pattern near the south pole is transferred to the tangent plane without much distortion, but the pattern near the north pole becomes severely distorted when it is transferred onto the plane that is tangent to the south pole. A line of latitude near the north pole, which is really a small circle on the surface of the sphere centered on the north pole, is mapped onto a huge circle on the tangent plane. (This huge circle is centered on the point that coincides with the south pole.) This example shows why a map of small areas near the south pole, when developed by using this technique, shows little distortion, and why the accuracy of the map begins to degrade as the surface being mapped begins to curve away from the tangent plane (see the accompanying illustration).

The process can be reversed as well. We can imagine a figure drawn on the plane. We place the south pole of the sphere on the point of the plane that is of most interest and repeat the construction described in the preceding paragraphs. This enables us to draw the plane figure onto the sphere, and in the neighborhood of the south pole there is little distortion. We can even trace the plane coordinate system onto the sphere along with the curve. In this way we can draw a coordinate system onto the surface of the sphere, and near the south pole the coordinate system will not be badly distorted. The main theme in all of this is that as the surface curves away from the tangent plane, the tangent plane becomes a poor approximation of the surface.

Gauss recognized that the study of curvature of the surface in the neighborhood of a point had to be understood in order to make much progress in the study of surfaces, and one of his important contributions to differential geometry was the study of curvature. Gauss found a way to measure the curvature of a surface in a way that would enable the user to state quantitatively exactly how curved a surface is. This is harder than it may first seem, because we often confuse the curvature of a surface with that of a curve.

A procedure for comparing the curvature of two plane curves is relatively simple to envision, although computing the curvature of a plane curve may require a fair amount of mathematics. We can compare the curvature of two plane curves at two points by simply superimposing the two points, one on top of the other, and then "tilting" one curve relative to the other until it becomes clear from inspection which of the two is more curved in the region of the point of interest. Intuitively at least the procedure is fairly clear. The additional problem presented by curved surfaces is that they can be curved in different directions at the same point. This is true for even very simple surfaces. The surface of a saddle, for example, is curved "up" when it is traversed from back to front and is curved "down" when it is traversed from side to side. As a consequence the curvature at any point on the axis of symmetry of the saddle is not entirely evident.

Gauss's solution to this was to reduce each three-dimensional problem of the curvature at a point on a surface to a set of two-dimensional problems involving curvatures of curves. To appreci-ate Gauss's idea, we begin by imagining a point, which we will call *P*, on a smooth surface. Now, imagine the tangent plane at *P*. (Recall that the tan-gent plane is the unique plane that is the best flat approxima-tion to the surface at the point of tangency.) Next imagine a line, which we call *l*, extending out of the surface at *P* and per-pendicular to the tangent plane. Now imagine a plane containing the line *l*. This sec-ond plane is perpendicular to the tangent plane and extends

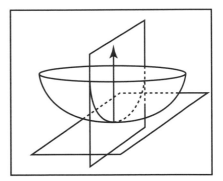

The intersection of a plane and a surface creates a curve. As the plane rotates about the arrow (vector) in the diagram, the curve determined by the surface and the plane also changes.

right through the surface. The line l forms a sort of hinge about which the plane can rotate.

No matter how we rotate the second plane about the line l, the intersection of this plane and the surface forms a curve through P. The shape of the curve usually depends on the orientation of the plane. Now imagine rotating this plane about line l. At each new position of the plane a new curve is formed by the intersection of the plane and the surface. In this way we form a set of curves containing the point P. For most surfaces of practical interest, there are a curve of greatest curvature and a curve of least curvature. One remarkable fact, discovered by Gauss, is that the direction of the curve with greatest curvature at P is always perpendicular to the direction of the curve of least curvature at P. Finally, Gauss computed the maximal and minimal curvatures at P and used the maximal and minimal curvatures to define something now known as the Gaussian curvature of the surface at the point.

Our description of Gauss's idea is rhetorical—expressed without equations—because the mathematics used in differential geometry is somewhat complex. Gauss, however, expressed his idea in the language of analysis. This is important, because in differential geometry a surface is described by one or more equations; the rhetorical descriptions used by the Greeks were no longer adequate. With just the equations to go on, the appearance of the surface may not be at all obvious. Nevertheless we can investigate its curvature by using Gauss's methods. This is part of the value of the analytical methods that Gauss helped pioneer.

The discovery of differential geometry allowed mathematicians to approach geometry from a different point of view. The tools of analysis made investigation of surfaces of increasing complexity possible. Mathematicians began to consider the problem of how to do mathematics on curved surfaces. For example, how can coordinate systems be imposed on curved surfaces? What are their properties? How are two different coordinate systems on a curved surface related to each other?

Coordinate systems and quantitative measures of the curvature of a surface were just the beginning. Mathematicians wanted to do mathematics on curved surfaces. They wanted to study curves and geometric figures on curved surfaces. For example, the curves might enclose regions of the (curved) surface. How could one compute the surface area enclosed by the curves? As Euler was, Gauss was interested in the problem of geodesics, the identification of the shortest path connecting two points on a curved surface. In ordinary two- or three-dimensional spaces a straight line is the shortest distance between two points, so, in a sense, on a curved surface geodesics are the analog to straight lines. These problems were not especially easy, but they, too, were just the beginning.

So far we have described the geometry of the surface as if we were standing on the outside looking in. Suppose, instead, that we were located on a very large curved surface from which we could not escape and out of which we could not see. We would, in effect, be two-dimensional beings. In this case the only geometry that we could know would be the geometry that occurred on the surface on which we lived. The only observations that we could make would be from the neighborhood of our position on the surface. This situation gives rise to many new questions: What could we learn about the surface on which we were located from observations made at the surface? Could we recognize, for example, whether or not the surface on which we lived were curved? Could we compute its curvature? These were new questions, and they provoked a lot of thought. One of the first mathematicians with answers was the German mathematician Bernard Riemann.

Georg Friedrich Bernhard Riemann

Georg Friedrich Bernhard Riemann, better known as Bernhard Riemann (1826–66), was one of the most imaginative mathematicians of the 19th century. He did not live a long life, dying of tuberculosis at 40. He did not publish many papers, and he had a very difficult time earning a living throughout much of his life. Nonetheless his mathematical insights were so striking that they permanently changed how mathematics was done.

Riemann was born into a family of modest means. All accounts of his early life indicate that his was a very close-knit family and

Bernhard Riemann. His geometric ideas helped prepare the way for the physics of the 20th century. (Library of Congress, Prints and Photographs Division)

that he remained close to his parents even after moving away. His father, a Lutheran minister, educated his son at home for several years before enrolling the boy in school. By the time Riemann had finished high school he had progressed beyond what his teachers could teach him. He seems to have especially enjoyed calculus and the theory of numbers.

It was the hope of his father that Riemann would study theology, and when Riemann entered university, he initially did just that. Soon, however, he wrote back to his father asking for permission to change his program of study so that he could concentrate on mathematics. His father agreed, and Riemann began his work in mathematics. As an undergraduate Riemann attended both Berlin University and the University of Göttingen, which was to 19th-century mathematics what Alexandria was to the mathematics of antiquity. It was from the University of Göttingen that Riemann eventually received a Ph.D. with Gauss as his thesis adviser. For years after obtaining his Ph.D. Riemann lived in poverty. During this time he produced several important mathematical papers.

Riemann's main achievements were in the areas of physics, geometry, number theory, complex variables, function theory, and differential equations. His writings were distinguished from those of most of his predecessors by the rhetorical way that he often expressed his ideas. In contrast to many of his contemporaries, who embraced the rigor that the new mathematics offered, Riemann generally avoided computation and extensive use of algebraic symbolism. His preference for prose rather than algebraic notation, and for intuition rather than strict rigor, was somewhat controversial at the time. Some mathematicians perceived his work—or at least the way that he expressed his work—as a step backward from the precision of Gauss and others. These objections have, for the most part, been forgotten because Riemann's insights have proved so useful.

In geometry Riemann began with the difficulties posed by Euclid's parallel postulate. Riemann, though a young man, was arriving late at the topic. That Euclid's parallel postulate was a stand-alone

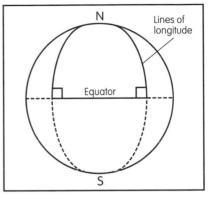

The triangle on the sphere formed by the equator and the two lines of longitude contains two right angles (located at the base of the triangle) and non-0 angle at the apex. This shows that the sum of the interior angles of the triangle exceeds 180°.

idea, independent of his other axioms and postulates, had already been demonstrated by Nikolai Lobachevsky and János Bolyai, as described earlier in this volume. Riemann, however, seems to have been unaware of their work. In any case his geometry was different from theirs. The alternatives to Euclid's fifth postulate proposed by Lobachevsky and Bolyai were roughly the same: Given a line and a point not on the line, there exist more than one line passing through the point parallel to the given line. Riemann, on the other hand, created another axiom entirely. In effect it said that given a line and a point not on the line there does not exist any line passing through the point and parallel to the given line. At first sight this axiom, too, seems counterintuitive, but Riemann's axiom is actually much easier to visualize than the axioms of Lobachevsky and Bolyai.

To visualize this idea, imagine doing geometry on a sphere instead of a plane—this is, after all, what mapmakers do every day. Define a great circle as the line on the sphere determined by the intersection of the sphere with any plane containing the center of the sphere. On a sphere these are the equivalent of straight lines. Every line of longitude, for example, is half of a great circle, because every line of longitude terminates at the poles. The equator is also a great circle. There are other great circles as well. For example, consider the great circle formed by "tipping" the equatorial plane (the plane that contains the equator) so that it contains both the center of the sphere and a point on the surface of the sphere that is at latitude 45°N: Half of the great circle is located above the equator; the other half is located below the equator.

To illustrate Riemann's axiom, choose a great circle passing through the poles: Call it L_1. If, now, we choose a point off L_1, any other great circle containing the point intersects our "line," L_1. To see this, suppose that we pass a line of longitude through the point. Call this line of longitude L_2. The great circle containing L_2 intersects L_1 at both the north and south poles of our sphere. On a sphere, where the great circles correspond to lines, there are no parallel lines.

Riemann's geometry has a number of peculiar properties when compared with Euclidean geometry. For example, the sum of the interior angles of a triangle exceeds 180°. To see how this can happen we return to doing geometry on a sphere. (The sphere is just a familiar example; Riemann's ideas are actually much more general than this.) Consider the triangle formed by the two lines of longitude and the equator. Each line of longitude crosses the equator at a right angle. Because the two lines of longitude meet at the north pole to form an angle whose measure is greater than 0, the sum of the interior angles of the triangle must exceed the sum of two right angles (see the sidebar Is Our World Euclidean? in chapter 7).

Riemann also generalized the geometry of ordinary Euclidean space, where we initially use the term *Euclidean space* for the so-called flat two- and three-dimensional spaces on which we impose a Cartesian coordinate system. Riemann extended this idea to spaces of four and more (generally n) dimensions. Points in n-dimensional space are placed in a one-to-one correspondence with "n-tuples" of real numbers $(x_1, x_2, x_3, \ldots, x_n)$. In this way we can impose a coordinate system on n-dimensional space.

Riemann also sought to imagine other types of spaces. He was especially interested in the idea of a curved space. Few, if any, of us can imagine what higher-dimensional curved spaces look like, so our intuition is of little value in trying to determine whether any of these spaces is flat or curved, or even whether the terms *flat* and *curved* have any meaning in these situations. Nevertheless space can be curved, and Riemann wanted a criterion that would enable him to determine whether a given space is curved or flat. He found the criterion that he was looking for, and it depends on the Pythagorean theorem.

Recall that the Pythagorean theorem in a Cartesian coordinate system in Euclidean space can be interpreted as a distance formula. If (x_1, y_1) and (x_2, y_2) are points in two-dimensional space, then the distance between the points is $\sqrt{(x_1 - x_2)^2 + (y_1 - y_2)^2}$. This formula generalizes easily to n-dimensional space. If $(x_1, x_2, x_3, \ldots, x_n)$ and $(y_1, y_2, y_3, \ldots, y_n)$ are two points in n-dimensional space, the distance between them is $\sqrt{(x_1 - y_1)^2 + (x_2 - y_2)^2 + (x_3 - y_3)^2 + \ldots + (x_n - y_n)^2}$. This looks more complicated than the two-dimensional case, but the idea, of course, is exactly the same. The only difference is that more terms are required to measure distance in n-dimensional space than in two-dimensional space.

Riemann said that regardless of the number of dimensions of the space, if the distance between the points in the space is given by the distance formula—that is, the generalized Pythagorean theorem—then the space is Euclidean. He called these spaces flat by analogy with a flat surface, for which the distance formula is easy to interpret as an application of the Pythagorean theorem.

Of course, none of this answers the question, What's the point? Why should we be concerned with the geometry of a space of dimension higher than 3? There are two answers to these questions. First, although our senses do not extend to higher-dimensional spaces, our imagination does. Mathematicians, scientists, and engineers frequently find it convenient and sometimes even necessary to compute in higher-dimensional spaces, as when they solve practical problems that involve many independent variables. These types of problems arise in fields as diverse as submarine navigation, stock market analysis, and meteorology, as well as a host of other fields. Understanding the geometric properties of higher-dimensional spaces is always helpful and sometimes vital in this regard.

Solving practical problems was not Riemann's goal, however. Riemann sought to understand geometry "from the inside." He was searching for a geometry that is intrinsic to the space, whether that space existed in two, three, or more dimensions. Happily what had already been discovered about two-dimensional surfaces could be applied (if not imagined) to spaces of higher dimensions. For example, we have (for the most part) described surfaces as if we were outside the surface looking in. From outside the surface we can easily observe several properties about the surface. From outside we can, for example, see whether the surface is curved. We can also observe whether the surface is of finite extent or whether the surface stretches on into infinity. Now imagine an imaginary creature living on this surface. Riemann wanted to know how this creature could determine the geometry of the surface *without making any measurements or observations from any point located off the surface.*

Riemann also thought beyond surfaces. He wanted, for example, to know how beings in a three-dimensional universe could determine the geometry of the universe in which they lived without making any measurements or observations from outside the universe. If this sounds too theoretical to be of value, remember that this is the sort of situation in which we find ourselves. There is no way that we can leave the universe to observe it from the outside. Any conclusions that we make about the geometry of space must, therefore, be made from inside. It was Riemann's hope that these investigations would eventually prove useful to science.

In his investigations of "geometry from the inside," Riemann imagined a system of geodesics. These would serve the same purpose in space as the coordinate lines that occur in flat, Euclidean space. A complete set of geodesics provided a coordinate system that would enable an imaginary being to find its way through space in just the same way, for example, that lines of longitude and latitude enable us to find our way about the globe. In Euclidean space the shortest distance between two points is a straight line; in a curved space the shortest distance between two points is a geodesic. Geodesics could be used to compute distances as well. To a creature inside the space, the system of geodesics would resemble Euclidean coordinates in the same way that near the point of tangency a surface resembles its tangent plane.

Could a creature living inside the space distinguish ordinary, three-dimensional Euclidean space (sometimes called flat space by analogy with the two-dimensional case) from curved space? Riemann's answer was yes. The curvature of space could be investigated from inside with the help of the Pythagorean theorem: If the distance between two points was not that predicted by the Pythagorean theorem, then the space was not Euclidean space. It had to be curved. In fact, the degree of curvature of the space could be investigated by noting how much the actual distances varied from those predicted by the Pythagorean theorem.

The curvature of space is important because of what it can mean about the size and shape of the universe. If space is infinite in extent, then it has no boundaries. In an infinite universe there can be no boundary with the property that if we pass through it, we will be "on the outside of it looking in." An infinite universe implies a universe without boundaries. The converse is, however, false. If we claim that the universe has no boundaries, it does not necessarily follow that the universe is infinite in extent.

Travel on the surface of the Earth illustrates this facet. In ages past there were many individuals who believed that Earth had edges (boundaries) such that if one traveled far enough in a straight line, one would fall off the edge. Not everyone believed this, of course. The Portuguese sailor and explorer Ferdinand Magellan (ca. 1480–1511) led an expedition that sailed continually westward. Not only did this group of explorers not fall off Earth, they eventually arrived back at their home port. This accomplishment was dramatic proof that Earth's surface has no boundaries. One can sail about the oceans forever, in any direction, and not fall off. This is a consequence of the curvature of Earth's surface: It has no boundaries or edges off which Magellan and his crew could fall. But Earth's surface is not infinite in extent, either. Any traveler proceeding in a straight line in any direction on Earth's surface eventually returns to his or her starting point, as Magellan's expedition did, because the surface of the Earth is finite in extent.

The reason this fact is important is that if space is curved, a similar sort of phenomenon can occur. By traveling along whatever the universe's equivalent of a great circle is, we would eventually, as Magellan's expedition did, arrive back at our starting point by moving continually forward. Riemann in a highly abstract way was dealing with some of the biggest of all scientific questions: What is the shape of the universe? How can we know our ideas are correct?

11

THE SHAPE OF SPACE
AND TIME

Many mathematicians found Riemann's ideas interesting and intellectually appealing, and Riemann's concepts led to a radical reassessment of geometry and the way to do geometry. It was Riemann's hope that these ideas would also further understanding in the physical sciences. Riemann's ideas eventually found application outside mathematics, but Riemann himself did not live long enough to see this occur. It was not long, however, before ideas about the curvature of space found their way into modern physics. Likewise, it was not long before the exotic geometries of Riemann began to appear better suited to describing the structure of the universe than the commonsense geometries of absolute space and absolute time that Newton had held dear.

The German-American physicist Albert Einstein (1879–1955) discovered that the geometry of the universe is substantially more complicated than that envisioned by Isaac Newton. His discoveries changed physicists' perceptions of space and time. Einstein was not a mathematician himself—in fact, he seemed never to tire of describing his difficulties with mathematics—but his discoveries added a great urgency to the study of differential geometry. A curved universe was no longer simply the imaginary home for an imaginary being; it was of interest to everyone. One hundred years after Einstein published his first paper on the subject of relativity, the ideas contained therein still spur research in the field of differential geometry.

Einstein was born in Germany. Throughout grammar school and high school he was an indifferent student, but he was fascinated with physics from an early age. In fact, as a youth he had two main interests: physics and music. His uncles introduced him to science and mathematics; his mother introduced him to music. Through good times and bad for the rest of his life he continued to play his violin and undertake research in physics—although not necessarily in that order.

Einstein attended college at the Federal Polytechnic Academy in Zürich, Switzerland. After graduation he became a Swiss citizen. He worked briefly as a high school mathematics teacher and eventually found work as a patent examiner, one who evaluates applications for patent protection. This job apparently was not very demanding of his time, and during his considerable free time he continued his research into physics. In 1905 he published four papers. One paper, on Brownian motion, enabled him to obtain a Ph.D. from the University of Zürich. Another paper on what has become known as the special theory of relativity changed scientists' ideas about the geometry of the universe and showed that the Newtonian reference frame was, for certain applications, not valid.

These papers attracted recognition from other scientists, though general public recognition was still some years off. He resigned his position as patent clerk and within the space of a few years taught at several European universities, among them his alma mater, the Federal Polytechnic Academy at Zürich, and later the University of Berlin. Einstein was in Berlin when World War I began, and he became involved in the antiwar movement. For much of his life Einstein used his position of prominence in an attempt to further his pacifist views. He was not very successful in this regard, and this was a source of personal disappointment and, occasionally, bitterness for him. As many other Jewish academics did, Einstein fled Germany shortly after the Nazis gained power in 1933. He made his way to the United States, where he settled in Princeton, New Jersey.

After Einstein attained prominence his interests shifted. He spent years arguing against many of the discoveries in the new branch of physics called quantum mechanics. Most physicists of the time acknowledged the value and importance of the new ideas that arose out of this field, but Einstein had difficulty accepting them. His efforts with respect to quantum mechanics bore no fruit. He is also remembered for having called to the attention of President Franklin Roosevelt the potentially dangerous implications of research that was being conducted in Europe on the splitting of the atom. In a letter sent to the president he described in general terms the possibility of using this new source of energy to create a new type of weapon. The letter was not Einstein's idea. Other scientists urged him to write it, but Einstein's prominence as a scientist caused Roosevelt to consider the possibility seriously. The eventual result was the Manhattan Project, the successful wartime effort by the United States to construct an atomic bomb. Einstein did not participate in the Manhattan Project himself.

Polar-ring galaxy (Courtesy of National Aeronautics and Space Administration)

After World War II, Einstein advocated the creation of a single world government to protect humanity from further large-scale conflict. His health declined. He died in his sleep in a hospital in Princeton.

Einstein's best-known contribution to science is, of course, the theory of relativity. (From long usage, relativity is still described as the theory of relativity, but so many of the predictions that arose out of Einstein's model of the universe have been confirmed that it is now a firmly established scientific fact.) Though the theory of relativity is, of course, related to physics, it is also a powerful statement about geometry. In classical physics the geometry of space and of time is considered to be as absolute as the laws of physics: The laws of physics as Newton understood them are everywhere the same, as is the geometry of space and time. This understanding began to change during the latter half of the 19th century.

Newton's ideas about the absolute nature of time and space had been called into question by a series of carefully conducted experiments by the German-born American physicist Albert Abraham Michelson and the American chemist Edward Williams Morley. The importance of what are now known as the Michelson–Morley experiments was recognized immediately. These experiments showed that it was not possible for *both* the laws of physics *and* the geometry of space and time to be absolute. Einstein's great accomplishment is that he argued that the laws of physics took precedence over the geometry of space and time that Newton envisioned. The result was the theory of relativity.

Geometry and the Special Theory of Relativity

Einstein's ideas on relativity are generally expressed in two parts, the theory of special relativity and the theory of general relativity. The theory of special relativity was published first. It is a nice application of two ideas that have played an important part in this history of geometry, coordinate systems and the geometry of right triangles. The theory of special relativity states that the laws of physics, including the speed of light, are the same for any reference frame (coordinate system) in uniform motion. (Uniform motion is motion along a straight line and at constant velocity.)

To see how this assertion destroys the geometry of time and space that Newton envisioned, we can perform a simple thought experiment. We imagine a rectangular box. We attach a laser to the top of the box and point it downward so that when the laser is turned on it illuminates the spot on the bottom of the box directly beneath it. We call the spot directly beneath the laser the target.

The speed of light is 300,000 kilometers per second (186,000 miles per hour), so the target is illuminated almost immediately after we turn on the laser, but *there is a small delay.* The light from the laser takes time to reach the bottom of the box. Because there is a delay, and because the speed of light in a vacuum is constant, we can use the laser as a sort of clock. We set one unit of time equal to the time the laser light takes to travel from the top of the box to the target below.

Now we imagine four things: (1) We imagine the box traveling along a straight line at constant speed. (2) We imagine turning

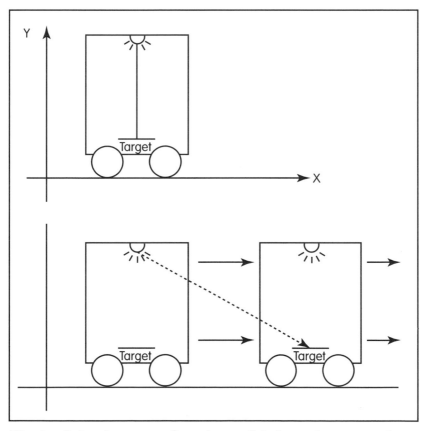

The time light takes to move from the top of the box to the target at the bottom can be used to calibrate a clock. We conclude that time passes at different rates for observers in different reference frames.

on the laser. (3) We imagine that we are inside the box watching the laser beam travel down from the top of the box to the target. (4) We imagine also watching the laser from a position outside the box and at rest as the box travels directly across our field of view.

If we were inside the box, our frame of reference would be the box itself. The origin of our coordinate system would be a point inside or on the box. This coordinate system would enable us to observe how things move relative to us and to the inside of the box. This is the "right" coordinate system for us because we are motionless relative to the box. In this coordinate frame, the time the laser takes to travel from the top of the box to the target is one unit of time. That unit of time is the same for the person inside the box no matter what the speed of the box, because according to the principle of special relativity, the speed of light is the same in any reference frame in uniform motion.

On the other hand, if we are positioned outside the box and motionless relative to the box, then as the box moves past us we see the tip of the laser beam follow a diagonal path as it travels from the top of the box to the target. The reason is that the box is not motionless relative to our outside-the-box coordinate system. If the laser followed a vertical path in our coordinate system then it would miss the target at the bottom of the box because the box had moved. If the box is moving to the right relative to our point of view, then the tip of the laser beam must also be moving to the right relative to our point of view; if it does not, it will miss the target, which is, after all, a moving target. These observations allow us to imagine a right triangle. The vertical side of the box constitutes one side of a right triangle. The distance traveled by the target from the time the laser was turned on until it was illuminated forms the second side of the triangle. The path of the tip of the laser beam forms the hypotenuse (see the diagram). Since the length of the hypotenuse is always longer than the length of either of the remaining sides, and since the speed of light is always the same for any frame of reference, the light took longer to reach the target *from our point of view outside the box*. (The diagonal distance traversed by the laser can be computed by using the Pythagorean theorem.) Since we were using the laser as a sort of clock, this shows that from the point of view of the observer who is standing still outside the box, time

THE PYTHAGOREAN THEOREM AND SPECIAL RELATIVITY

Finding out how much more slowly time inside the moving box passes relative to time outside the box requires only the Pythagorean theorem, one of the oldest formulas in geometry. First, we compute how long the horizontal and vertical legs of the triangle described in the main body of the text are. Let t represent the time required for the laser light to travel from the top of the box to the bottom, where t is measured from inside the box. Let $\bar{t}$ represent the time the light takes to move from the top of the box to the bottom as measured from outside the box. Our goal is to compute t in terms of $\bar{t}$.

Let v represent the speed with which the box moves to the right. The distance the box moves to the right between the time the laser is fired and the time it strikes the target is easily computed: It is $v\bar{t}$. The height of the box can also be computed in terms of time. Because light always travels at constant speed—we let the letter C represent the speed of light—the distance from the top to the bottom of the box in both coordinate systems is Ct. The length of the hypotenuse is $C\bar{t}$, the speed of light multiplied by the time it takes for the laser to hit the target as measured from outside the box. The three lengths, $C\bar{t}$, $v\bar{t}$, and Ct, are all related through Pythagoras's theorem: $C^2\bar{t}^2 = v^2\bar{t}^2 + C^2t^2$. We use a little algebra to solve this equation for t. The result is $t = \bar{t}\sqrt{1 - v^2/C^2}$. This shows that time inside the box passes more slowly relative to time in the coordinate system for the observer located outside the box, and that we can make it pass as slowly as we please provided we make v, the speed of the box, large enough. When v is about $0.87C$, or about 87 percent of the speed of light, time inside the box is elapsing at only half the rate of the time in the coordinate system for the observer situated outside the box.

It must be kept in mind that this is a change in time itself. It has nothing to do with a mechanical effect on clocks. Time itself is elapsing at a different rate inside the box than it is outside the box, and this is a purely logical consequence of the assertion that the laws of physics (including the speed of light) are the same in every frame of reference moving along a straight line at constant velocity.

THE GEOMETRY AND SCIENCE OF "ORDINARY" SURFACES

Differential geometry is often associated with the theory of relativity. The theory of relativity makes a number of very spectacular and unexpected predictions about the shape of the universe, and these predictions are made in the language of differential geometry. Relativity is a famous, if not widely understood, theory. But the study of curved surfaces has proved to be important in other areas as well. One important application concerns the physics of surface flow.

Most "hands-on" science museums now have something called a bubble hoist. It consists of a rectangular frame, a bar, cables, and a trough of prepared liquid. The cables are attached to both ends of the frame and threaded through small holes in the bar. The bar is lowered

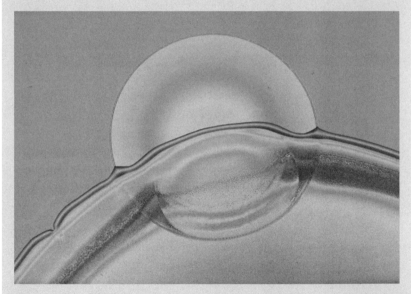

The study of the geometry and of the dynamics of flows inside membranes has become an important branch of applied mathematics. (CORBIS)

inside the box is passing more slowly than time outside it. (To compute how much more slowly, see The Pythagorean Theorem and Special Relativity.)

into the trough by a rope, and when it is pulled up, usually by means of a rope, it draws up a large soapy film after it. The film extends from one cable to the other and from the bar to the trough. It is thinner than a hair, and, in particular, it is millions of times thinner than it is wide or tall. Close inspection of the bubble reveals that it is not static. Fluid is flowing down the film in a complicated pattern.

Complicated two-dimensional flows can sometimes be described by using the ordinary flat Cartesian coordinate system with which we are familiar, but in this case there are complications that make this impossible. The membrane is very flexible. A slight breeze causes it to bend. Small vibrations of the frame are transmitted to the membrane through the bar and cables. The two-dimensional surface of the membrane responds to these forces by deforming. The forces that hold the membrane together are exerted from inside the surface, and the strength of these forces is determined in part by the curvature of the surface. Meanwhile the motion of the fluids inside the membrane is continually responding to the curvature of the surface. Successful models of these types of phenomena must be built on a geometry that is intrinsic to the surface. In other words scientists need the more sophisticated geometry pioneered by Bernhard Riemann to describe the physics of flow within the bubble hoist.

The range of problems that use these geometric ideas is now quite wide. For example, when two immiscible liquids, such as oil and water, contact each other, they interact across a surface of constantly changing shape. Understanding the dynamics of the interface between these two fluids is important if one wants to control processes that involve two nonmixing fluids. Another example of a phenomenon that is sometimes modeled by using geometric methods that are intrinsic to the surface is flame-front propagation. In this model the flame is the interface between two different materials: the reactants, which are the chemicals that are to be burned, and the products, which are the chemicals produced by the combustion reaction. Almost any process that involves two separate materials separated by a surface can benefit from this type of analysis. Riemann would almost certainly be pleased that the highly abstract problems with which he grappled almost a century and a half ago are now applied to such practical problems.

The words *slowly* and *quickly* are relative terms, of course. To the person inside the box, everything is just as it should be. The laser still takes exactly one unit of time to leave the top of the box and hit the target on the floor. This cannot change because (according to the theory of special relativity) the speed of light is the same in every reference frame in uniform motion.

In the same way that the passage of time can be different for different observers, distance, too, is different for observers in different reference frames. This should not be surprising. If time can dilate, then we should expect changes in distance as well. (In our own experience we often assume the equivalency of time and distance. Whenever we describe a location as a two-hour drive away, we are substituting a time measurement for a distance measurement.)

To see how distances, too, can be different for different observers imagine two planets in space that are not moving relative to each other. Suppose that, from the point of view of a creature on one of the planets, the planets are one light-year apart. (A light-year is the distance that light travels in a single year.) So from the creature's point of view, travel from one planet to the next must always take at least a year, because nothing travels faster than the speed of light. But time passes more slowly for the passenger inside a rocket traveling between the two planets than for an observer situated on one of the planets, for the same reason that time passes more slowly for the observer in the box described earlier than for the observer in the coordinate system outside the box. Furthermore the faster one travels, the more slowly time inside the rocket passes relative to time on the planet. This means that from the point of view of someone inside the rocket, travel from one planet to the next might take only six months. This cannot mean that the rocket is traveling faster than the speed of light, because (again) nothing goes faster than the speed of light. It can only mean that from the point of view of someone inside the rocket the two planets are less than one-half light-year apart. The faster one goes relative to the speed of light, the shorter distances become. The simple-sounding statement "The laws of physics are the same for any frame of reference that moves at constant speed along a straight line" implies that neither time nor space is absolute. There is no escaping it: The geometry of the universe is more complicated than it first seemed; the geometry of the universe is flexible.

Einstein's discoveries in special relativity are surprising to most people. The reason is that his results depend on the speed of light. Travel at speeds that are near the speed of light is completely outside our ordinary experience. Because we move so slowly relative to the speed of light the changes predicted by the theory of relativity are so small that we cannot detect them. They are so small that no one knew about them until Einstein deduced their existence, although the relative dilation of time and space occurs whenever one observer moves relative to another.

Einstein later published his general theory of relativity. The general theory shows that space and time are even more flexible than his special theory indicated. The geometry of the universe could be not only dilated but also curved. Riemann had wanted to know how much an imaginary being living upon a curved surface could discover about the surface without stepping outside it. His questions were now of interest to scientists as well as mathematicians. Scientists now wanted to know about the geometric structure of the universe, too. Einstein indicated that space could be curved, but how curved is it, and in what direction is it curved? These are questions that are still being investigated.

Emmy Noether and Symmetry

Einstein is sometimes described as a kind of scientific prophet, leading his fellow physicists to a new, relativistic universe. It is worth remembering, however, that at the time of his discoveries Einstein was not the only one searching for a satisfactory explanation to the experiments of Michelson and Morley. He was not alone in recognizing that the old concepts did not adequately explain the new data, and he was not alone in suspecting that Michelson and Morley's experiment pointed the way toward the next Big Idea in physics.

To be sure Einstein was the person first to propose the theory of relativity, but he was not so far ahead of his time that his ideas were unappreciated. Many other physicists and mathematicians quickly recognized the validity of his discoveries. This does not always occur with important discoveries. There have been scientists and mathematicians who were so far ahead of their time that their contributions were not recognized until long after their death. It was otherwise with Einstein. Both the theory of relativity and its principal theorist were widely celebrated within a few years after Einstein began publishing his ideas.

As Einstein's fellow scientists have, the popular press has always accorded the theory of relativity a good deal of attention. On the one hand this is surprising. The dilations of time and space that are predicted by the theory only become easily noticeable under conditions that are far beyond ordinary human experience. Despite all the descriptions so regularly recounted in newspapers and magazines of identical twins moving at different speeds and aging at different rates, no human has ever traveled relative to another human at a speed that is a significant fraction of the speed of light. No country has plans to accelerate an astronaut or cosmonaut to such speeds at any time in the foreseeable future. The practical difficulties involved in attaining such speeds (and then slowing down) are enormous.

In many ways the theory of relativity is old news, but even its most basic predictions continue to fascinate both the trained scientist and the interested layperson. Part of the reason for this continued interest must be that the theory predicts that time and space are mutable. Geometry, according to Einstein, is not quite as fundamental as most of us are still led to believe.

To the ancient Greeks there was no physics in the modern sense. They learned about nature through geometry. Science in ancient Greece was applied geometry. Devoid of the concepts of force, mass, and energy, the Greeks saw geometry as the central organizing principle of nature. Later Galileo, Isaac Newton, and others saw geometry and physics as complementary. There are laws—physical laws—governing the motion of bodies, but these motions and the laws that describe them exist in a geometric context, the geometry of absolute time and space described by Newton. It was Einstein who asserted that there were circumstances in which the laws of geometry (as they had been understood since antiquity) and the laws of physics sometimes conflict.

It was part of his great discovery that when a conflict arises between physics and geometry, physics prevails. Distances change, time dilates, but the speed of light remains constant. This idea was surprising when Einstein first discovered it, and it continues to surprise most of us today.

It may seem geometry had been "dethroned" from the place it had occupied in the human imagination for millennia, and in some ways this is exactly what had happened. But the idea of geometry as a central organizing principle of nature was successfully reintroduced not long after Einstein published his paper on the general theory of relativity in 1915. (General relativity is an extension of the ideas of special relativity, the relativity described in the previous section.) The person to reestablish the importance of geometry as an organizing principle in nature was the German mathematician Emmy Noether (1882–1935).

Noether grew up in Erlangen, Germany, the daughter of the prominent mathematician Max Noether, a professor at Erlangen University. As a youth the younger Noether showed facility with languages, and her original goal was to teach foreign languages in secondary schools. To that end she received certification as a teacher in English and French, but she never taught languages. Instead she began to study advanced mathematics.

Higher mathematics was a difficult career path for a woman in Germany at this time. A woman could take university-level courses, but only with the permission of the instructor. Furthermore it was a general rule that women were barred from taking the exams that would enable them to become faculty members at universities. This was the situation in which Noether found herself.

Noether eventually received a Ph.D. in 1907 from the University of Erlangen, and for a while she remained at Erlangen and taught an occasional class for her father, but she did so without pay. She continued her studies and eventually drew the attention of David Hilbert and Fritz Klein at Göttingen University. Noether moved to Göttingen in 1915. Although Klein and Hilbert advocated that the university offer her a position on the faculty, this was initially denied. Other faculty members objected to the hiring of women. Nevertheless Noether began to teach an occasional course under David Hilbert's name. As she became better known, mathematicians from outside the university began to sit in on the classes that she taught. In 1919 she was offered a position at Göttingen. Noether remained at the university until 1933, when she and the other Jewish faculty members were fired from their positions. She then moved to the United States, where she taught at the Princeton Institute for Advanced Studies, Princeton, New Jersey, and Bryn Mawr College, Bryn Mawr, Pennsylvania, until her death of complications associated with surgery.

To appreciate Noether's contributions to geometry some knowledge of conservation laws is helpful. A conservation law is a statement that a certain property—energy, for example—is conserved. The word *conserved* has a very special usage in this situation. It means that in a system that is isolated from its environment—by sealing the material of interest inside a test tube, for example—the total amount of the conserved property cannot change. Mass, momentum, and energy are all examples of conserved properties. More generally if the system is not isolated from the environment then we should be able to keep track of changes in the (conserved) property by measuring how much crosses the boundary of the system. *Because* the property is conserved, the only way that the property inside the system can increase is if more of it enters the system from the outside; the only way it can decrease is if some crosses the boundary of the system on its way outside.

Consider the example of conservation of mass. It is a basic tenet of classical physics that mass is conserved over the course of a chemical reaction. In other words if we cause a chemical reaction to occur inside a sealed test tube, then the mass of the material in the tube before the reaction equals the mass of the material in the tube after the reaction. (This is what *conserved* means.) In particular if we want to diminish the mass in the tube, then we must allow some of the material in the tube to cross the boundary of the tube; that is just a formal way of stating that if we want the mass to diminish we have to take something out of the tube. We cannot simply make what is in the tube disappear.

When Einstein first proposed his ideas about relativity, there were questions among some scientists about whether energy is conserved in Einstein's theory. (It has been a basic tenet of science since the middle of the 19th century that energy is a conserved property.) If it could be shown that energy would not be conserved, then the correctness of Einstein's ideas would be called into question. Hilbert, who was very interested in relativity, was unable to resolve the issue of energy conservation. He asked Emmy Noether to investigate the problem.

Noether quickly responded with some fundamental observations about the nature of conservation laws in general. She discovered that there exists a very close relationship between conservation laws, which for centuries have been the fundamental concepts on which Western science is based, and the geometric principle of symmetry.

In geometry symmetry is an important organizing principle, and certain types of symmetry are familiar to us all. The bodies of most people are almost perfectly symmetric. The left half of the body is the mirror image (more or less) of the right half. The term for this is *bilateral symmetry*. Other types of symmetry are possible. For example, a cylinder is rotationally symmetric about the line that passes through the axis of symmetry of the cylinder: No matter how we rotate the cylinder about the line, the position in space occupied by the cylinder itself is unchanged. Ideas about symmetry have been generalized over the years so that mathematicians can talk about several different types of symmetry, some of which are easier to appreciate than others.

To return to the cylinder described in the pervious paragraph, suppose we form a set consisting of every geometric transformation of the cylinder that leaves its spatial configuration unchanged. (Geometric transformations are described in chapter 6.) As indicated in the previous paragraph, we can rotate the cylinder about its line of symmetry and it will occupy the same position in space after the rotation as it did before the rotation took place, so rotations belong to this set of transformations.

Next, consider the reflection of the cylinder about the plane that passes through the center of the cylinder and is perpendicular to the cylinder's axis of symmetry. This transformation produces a "mirror image" of the cylinder, and it, too, belongs to our set. And we can do more: If we choose any two symmetry transformations of the cylinder and combine them by performing first one transformation on the cylinder and then the other—this is called a product of the transformations—then we obtain still another symmetry transformation. In fact, the set of such symmetry transformations on the cylinder forms a group. The existence of such symmetry groups and their logical structure is as important in physics as in mathematics.

What Noether discovered is that each conservation law is an assertion about a particular kind of symmetry, and, conversely, each symmetry group present in a system of equations indicates a certain type of conservation law. For example, one consequence of Noether's discovery is that the assertion that energy is conserved is also an assertion about symmetry with respect to time. To see why this is so, imagine time as a line. We can imagine translating ourselves forward or backward along this line and occasionally pausing to look at a particular isolated system. The statement that energy is conserved is an assertion that no matter where we find ourselves along the time line, the energy of that isolated system is the same in the past as it is in the future. Like a mirror image, the condition of the system is the same on both sides of our position on the line no matter where we choose to stop. In fact, the principle of conservation of energy is valid if and only if this kind of symmetry with respect to time holds: In other words if the symmetry condition holds, then no matter how we divide the timeline, the energy on one side of the divide (say the "future" side) is the mirror image of the energy on the other (past) side. Conversely if energy is conserved the symmetry with respect to time must hold as well.

We can even summarize Einstein's special theory of relativity simply by saying that it is the statement that the laws of physics are invariant with respect to a group called the Poincaré group of symmetry transformations.

Noether's observations about the role of symmetry in physics restored geometry as an organizing principle in science. Although it is true that the laws of physics prevail over the old ideas of absolute time and absolute space, it is now known to be true that the laws of physics are themselves expressions of certain geometric principles. Geometric symmetries and laws of nature cannot be viewed as competing concepts. The truth of the laws depends on the validity of the symmetries, and the validity of the symmetries assures the truth of the laws.

12

INFINITE-DIMENSIONAL GEOMETRY

Our intuition is often a useful guide for understanding geometry in two and three dimensions, a fact well illustrated by the investigations of Greek geometers. In the 19th century Riemann extended geometry from two- and three-dimensional spaces to spaces of higher dimension. Imagining the geometry of four-, five-, and higher-dimensional spaces is more challenging, but many of the properties of spaces of two and three dimensions carry over directly to spaces of higher dimensions as Riemann showed. All of the spaces that Riemann considered, however, were finite-dimensional: That is, the spaces had a limited—though perhaps a very large—number of dimensions. The restriction to finite-dimensional spaces was lifted in the 20th century when some mathematicians began the study of spaces of infinitely many dimensions.

Much of the motivation to create and study infinite-dimensional spaces arises out of the need to understand sets of functions. The study of abstract sets of functions is called functional analysis. It was pioneered by the German mathematician and physicist David Hilbert (1852–1943), and many of the most common infinite-dimensional spaces are today classified as Hilbert spaces.

Hilbert was one of the most versatile and influential mathematicians of the 20th century. Although he died before the middle of the century, his influence extended throughout the century. Hilbert's hometown was Königsberg, now Kaliningrad. He attended university there, and after he received a Ph.D. he remained for several more years to teach. Eventually as many of the main figures in the history of geometry did, Hilbert joined the faculty at Göttingen, where he remained for the rest of his life.

Hilbert made a number of important contributions to several areas of mathematics and physics. He developed the so-called field equations for relativity theory—equations that are the mathematical expression of the ideas of relativity theory—at about the same time that Einstein did. He made important contributions to other branches of physics as well. He also made important discoveries in algebra, and he developed a complete, logically consistent set of axioms for Euclidean

David Hilbert, one of the most influential mathematicians of the 20th century (Baldwin G. Ward & Kathryn C. Ward/CORBIS)

geometry. His influence on later generations of mathematicians stems from a series of problems that he formulated in 1900. In an address to a mathematical congress in Paris, he described those problems that he believed would be important to the development of mathematics in the new century. His speech placed these 23 problems right at the center of mathematical research. Hilbert's choice of problems helped to guide mathematical research throughout the century, though there can be little doubt that his own professional prestige also drew attention to the list and caused the problems to be taken more seriously than they otherwise would have been.

Hilbert spaces, the infinite-dimensional spaces of most interest to us in this volume, sound exotic. In some ways they are. Infinite-dimensional spaces have a number of properties that make them different from finite-dimensional spaces. Nevertheless many of the basic properties of Hilbert spaces are relatively straightforward generalizations of the properties of the "flat," finite-dimensional spaces that we have already encountered. To study a Hilbert space, for example, we first need a method that enables us to "find our way around": to this end we need to introduce a coordinate system. Recall that in the study of two-dimensional spaces, mathematicians associate an ordered pair of numbers, (x_1, x_2), with each point in space. In three-dimensional spaces mathematicians associate an ordered triplet, (x_1, x_2, x_3), with each point in space. More generally in n-dimensional space, where n can represent any natural number, we establish a correspondence between points in space and ordered n-tuples, $(x_1, x_2, x_3, x_4, \ldots, x_n)$. In accordance with this pattern, each point in the Hilbert spaces we consider can be placed in correspondence with an ordered, infinite sequence of numbers, $(x_1, x_2, x_3, x_4, \ldots)$, although, as we will soon see, the generalization is not quite so straightforward as it might first appear.

Having established position in this infinite-dimensional space, we must find a way of measuring distances. Again we can look to finite-dimensional spaces for guidance. In two-dimensional space the distance between any two points, (x_1, x_2) and (y_1, y_2), is given by the Pythagorean theorem: $\sqrt{(x_1 - y_1)^2 + (x_2 - y_2)^2}$. In n-dimensional space the distance between any two points, $(x_1, x_2, x_3, x_4, \ldots, x_n)$ and $(y_1, y_2, y_3, y_4, \ldots, y_n)$, is defined by using a generalization of the Pythagorean theorem: $\sqrt{(x_1 - y_1)^2 + (x_2 - y_2)^2 + \ldots + (x_n - y_n)^2}$. In an infinite-dimensional space the distance between the points $(x_1, x_2, x_3, x_4, \ldots)$ and $(y_1, y_2, y_3, y_4, \ldots)$ is again given by a straightforward extension of the Pythagorean theorem: $\sqrt{(x_1 - y_1)^2 + (x_2 - y_2)^2 + \ldots}$.

An important difference between finite-dimensional and infinite-dimensional spaces arises when we try to apply the distance formula. In an n-dimensional Euclidean space, where n represents any natural number, any collection of n numbers identifies a point in the space. For example, the point $(x_1, x_2, x_3, x_4, \ldots, x_n)$ is located at a distance $\sqrt{x_1^2 + x_2^2 + \ldots + x_n^2}$ from the origin. The situation is more complicated for a Hilbert space. To observe the difference let $(x_1, x_2, x_3, x_4, \ldots)$ represent a possible point in a Hilbert space. Consider $\sqrt{x_1^2 + x_2^2 + x_3^2 + \ldots}$, an expression that purports to represent the distance from the origin of coordinates—the origin has coordinates $(0, 0, 0, \ldots)$—to the point $(x_1, x_2, x_3, x_4, \ldots)$. It is quite possible that the sum underneath the square root sign "diverges," that is, the sum becomes larger than any number that we can imagine provided we add enough terms in the series. On the other hand, the sum may "converge"; that means that no matter how many terms in the sum we add together, our answer remains smaller than some fixed number. Under these latter circumstances the "infinite sum" under the square root sign represents some number. If the sum inside the square root sign converges, then the point $(x_1, x_2, x_3, x_4, \ldots)$ belongs to the Hilbert space. If, however, the sum diverges, then we conclude the corresponding infinite sequence of numbers does not represent a point in Hilbert space. There are many infinite sequences of numbers that cannot be placed in correspondence with points in a Hilbert space. The point $(1, 1, 1, \ldots)$ is an example of such a sequence.

Having established both a coordinate system and a way to compute distances, we can begin discussing the geometry of infinite-dimensional space. There are infinite-dimensional spheres, lines, and so forth—though of course, for most of us, imagining what these might look like is impossible. There is, however, a way around our inability to "see" in spaces of infinite dimension. One key to doing geometry in infinite-dimensional spaces is to choose our descriptions of objects so that they apply to spaces of any number of dimensions. Once this has been done we can use our three-dimensional intuition to guide our infinite-dimensional understanding.

Consider the example of a sphere. In three-dimensional space a sphere is completely described once its radius and the location of its center are specified: Let the letter r represent the radius, and describe the sphere with radius r and center at the origin as "the set of all points that are at a distance r from the origin." Notice that in this definition we do not mention anything about the dimension of the space; we use only the facts that the space has an origin and a distance function. Because our three-dimensional definition does not depend on the dimension of the space, we can use the same definition of a sphere for every other space with an origin and a distance function. Our definition even works in an infinite-dimensional space: "The set of all points that are at a distance r from the origin" is a complete description of an infinite-dimensional sphere of radius r centered at the origin. Other surfaces and properties can be defined in a similar way.

None of this, of course, indicates why anyone would want to study infinite-dimensional spaces. Much of the value of infinite-dimensional spaces is that they enable the user to understand functions in a new way. In this very broad viewpoint functions are pictured as "points" in space. This type of description offers a new way of thinking about functions. Such "function spaces" enable the user to bring much of what has been learned about the geometry of Euclidean space to bear on the analysis of functions and sets of functions. We can discuss the distance between functions, the geometry of certain sets of functions, and many other more abstract properties in much the same way that we are taught to study sets of points in three-dimensional space. The ability to use this type of analysis is important because it often provides mathematicians with a useful context for analyzing a function or class of functions.

Before the development of Hilbert spaces progress in understanding large sets of functions was slow. Each set had to be analyzed individually. Many of these sets could, in fact, be modeled as subsets of a Hilbert space, but this potential was not yet recognized. Without a conceptual framework the relations between the different sets of functions was not clear. There was no unity to the subject. With the invention of Hilbert spaces mathematicians could reframe specific questions about sets of functions in terms of the general geometry of Hilbert spaces. The results they obtained through the study of Hilbert spaces could then be applied to many specific classes of functions. This development gave conceptual unity to a wide and previously fragmented field. Functional analysis, of which the study of infinite-dimensional function spaces is only a part, has proved to be an important branch of mathematics with applications to the sciences as well as other branches of mathematics.

Hilbert spaces are only one type of infinite-dimensional space. There are many others, each of which has its own distinct mathematical properties. Some of these other spaces are named after their founders. For example, two of the most widely studied spaces are Banach spaces, named after the Austro-Hungarian–born mathematician Stefan Banach (1892–1945), and Sobolev spaces, named after the Russian mathematician Sergei Lvovich Sobolev (1908–89). Other widely studied infinite-dimensional spaces have more utilitarian-sounding names, for example, nuclear spaces and distributional spaces. All of these spaces were invented (or discovered, depending on one's point of view) in response to specific mathematical problems. Having become acquainted with these spaces, however, many mathematicians became fascinated with their properties as mathematical objects. Some of these mathematicians now study infinite dimensional spaces for their intrinsic interest in just the same way that Greek mathematicians studied Euclidean geometry more than 2,000 years ago: Contemporary mathematicians seek to classify these spaces and to ask and answer questions that reveal important structural properties possessed by each type of space. Although the mathematical subject matter has changed, the spirit of mathematical curiosity that motivates these mathematicians is the same one that motivated Apollonius, Euclid, and Archimedes so many years ago.

The existence of so many infinite-dimensional spaces is, however, also a reflection of their utility outside of mathematics. Mathematicians and physicists have now learned how to use specific spaces to ask a variety of important questions in the physical sciences. Solutions to problems in the flow of turbulent fluids, shockwaves, and the inner structure of the atom, for example, have sometimes depended on insight into the nature of infinite-dimensional spaces. Research into infinite-dimensional spaces began early in the 20th century, and it remains an active area of inquiry today.

Infinite-dimensional spaces are only one example of the most recent extensions of the concepts of geometry to ever more exotic spaces. Over the course of thousands of years the straightedge and compass constructions of the ancient Greeks—carried out on flat stones sprinkled with sand—gave way to alternative geometries, geometries in higher-dimensional spaces, and an ever-increasing level of abstraction. But Euclidean geometry, the geometry of the ancient Greeks, remains with us. It forms an important part of every student's mathematical education, and it is used extensively in many scientific and engineering disciplines. Most importantly the geometric ideas of Euclid—though they have been generalized, modified, and refined by his successors well past a point at which Euclid would recognize his own handiwork—have not been abandoned by the mathematicians of today. The Pythagorean theorem, axiomatic reasoning, and the concept of a point remain as important in higher mathematics as they were in Euclid's time. This unity of subject does not exist for every branch of higher mathematics. There are other types of mathematics that have been entirely transformed. These disciplines—algebra is but one example—have nothing in common with their historical roots but a name. Geometry, on the other hand, has evolved without losing its emphasis on lines, surfaces, and shapes. It is still an expression of the way we see the world.

CHRONOLOGY

ca. 3000 B.C.E.
Hieroglyphic numerals are in use in Egypt.

ca. 2500 B.C.E.
Construction of the Great Pyramid of Khufu takes place.

ca. 2400 B.C.E.
An almost complete system of positional notation is in use in Mesopotamia.

ca. 1800 B.C.E.
The Code of Hammurabi is promulgated.

ca. 1650 B.C.E.
The Egyptian scribe Ahmes copies what is now known as the Ahmes (or Rhind) papyrus from an earlier version of the same document.

ca. 1200 B.C.E.
The Trojan War is fought.

ca. 740 B.C.E.
Homer composes the *Odyssey* and the *Iliad*, his epic poems about the Trojan War.

ca. 585 B.C.E.
Thales of Miletus carries out his research into geometry, marking the beginning of mathematics as a deductive science.

ca. 540 B.C.E.
Pythagoras of Samos establishes the Pythagorean school of philosophy.

ca. 500 B.C.E.
Rod numerals are in use in China.

ca. 420 B.C.E.
Zeno of Elea proposes his philosophical paradoxes.

ca. 399 B.C.E.
Socrates dies.

ca. 360 B.C.E.
Eudoxus, author of the method of exhaustion, carries out his research into mathematics.

ca. 350 B.C.E.
The Greek mathematician Menaechmus writes an important work on conic sections.

ca. 347 B.C.E.
Plato dies.

332 B.C.E.
Alexandria, Egypt, is established. It will become the center of Greek mathematics.

ca. 300 B.C.E.
Euclid of Alexandria writes *Elements*, one of the most influential mathematics books of all time.

ca. 260 B.C.E.
Aristarchus of Samos discovers a method for computing the ratio of the Earth–Moon distance to the Earth–Sun distance.

ca. 230 B.C.E.
Eratosthenes of Cyrene computes the circumference of Earth.

Apollonius of Perga writes *Conics*.

Archimedes of Syracuse writes *The Method*, *Equilibrium of Planes*, and other works.

206 B.C.E.
The Han dynasty is established; Chinese mathematics flourishes.

ca. C.E. 150
Ptolemy of Alexandria writes *Almagest*, the most influential astronomy text of antiquity.

ca. C.E. 250

Diophantus of Alexandria writes *Arithmetica*, an important step forward for algebra.

ca. 320

Pappus of Alexandria writes his *Collection*, one of the last influential Greek mathematical treatises.

415

The death of the Alexandrian philosopher and mathematician Hypatia marks the end of the Greek mathematical tradition.

ca. 476

The astronomer and mathematician Aryabhata is born; Indian mathematics flourishes.

ca. 630

The Hindu mathematician and astronomer Brahmagupta writes *Brahma-sphuta-siddhānta*, which contains a description of place-value notation.

641

The Library of Alexandria is burned.

ca. 775

Scholars in Baghdad begin to translate Hindu and Greek works into Arabic.

ca. 830

Mohammed ibn-Mūsā al-Khwārizmī writes *Hisāb al-jabr wa'l muqābala*, a new approach to algebra.

833

Al-Ma'mūn, founder of the House of Wisdom in Baghdad (now Iraq), dies.

ca. 840

The Jainist mathematician Mahavira writes *Ganita Sara Samgraha*, an important mathematical textbook.

1071

William the Conqueror quells the last of the English rebellions.

1086

An intensive survey of the wealth of England is carried out and summarized in the tables and lists of the *Domesday Book*.

1123

Omar Khayyám, author of *Al-jabr w'al muqābala* and the *Rubáiyát*, the last great classical Islamic mathematician, dies.

ca. 1144

Bhaskara II writes the *Lilavati* and the *Vija-Ganita*, two of the last great works in the classical Indian mathematical tradition.

ca. 1202

Leonardo of Pisa (Fibonacci), author of *Liber Abaci*, arrives in Europe.

1360

Nicholas Oresme, French mathematician and Roman Catholic bishop, represents distance as the area beneath a velocity line.

1471

The German artist Albrecht Dürer is born.

1482

Leonardo da Vinci begins to keep his diaries.

ca. 1541

Niccolò Fontana, an Italian mathematician, also known as Tartaglia, discovers a general method for factoring third-degree algebraic equations.

1543

Copernicus publishes *De Revolutionibus*, marking the start of the Copernican revolution.

1545

Girolamo Cardano, an Italian mathematician and physician, publishes *Ars Magna*, marking the beginning of modern algebra. Later he publishes *Liber de Ludo Aleae*, the first book on probability.

ca. 1554

Sir Walter Raleigh, explorer, adventurer, amateur the mathematician, and patron of the mathematician Thomas Harriot, is born.

1579

François Viète, a French mathematician, publishes *Canon Mathematicus*, marking the beginning of modern algebraic notation.

1585

The Dutch mathematician and engineer Simon Stevin publishes "La disme."

1609

Johannes Kepler, author of Kepler's laws of planetary motion, publishes *Astronomia Nova*.

Galileo Galilei begins his astronomical observations.

1621

The English mathematician and astronomer Thomas Harriot dies. His only work, *Artis Analyticae Praxis*, is published in 1631.

ca. 1630

The French lawyer and mathematician Pierre de Fermat begins a lifetime of mathematical research. He is the first person to claim to have proved Fermat's last theorem.

1636

Gérard (also Girard or Gaspard) Desargues, a French mathematician and engineer, publishes *Traité de la section perspective*, which marks the beginning of projective geometry.

1637

René Descartes, a French philosopher and mathematician, publishes *Discours de la méthode*, permanently changing both algebra and geometry.

1638

Galileo Galilei publishes *Dialogues Concerning Two New Sciences* while under arrest.

1640

Blaise Pascal, a French philosopher, scientist, and mathematician, publishes *Essai sur les coniques*, an extension of the work of Desargues.

1642

Blaise Pascal manufactures an early mechanical calculator, the Pascaline.

1648

The Thirty Years' War, a series of conflicts that involves much of Europe, ends.

1649

Oliver Cromwell takes control of the English government after a civil war.

1654

Pierre de Fermat and Blaise Pascal exchange a series of letters about probability, thereby inspiring many mathematicians to study the subject.

1655

John Wallis, an English mathematician and clergyman, publishes *Arithmetica Infinitorum*, an important work that presages calculus.

1657

Christian Huygens, a Dutch mathematician, astronomer, and physicist, publishes *De Ratiociniis in Ludo Aleae*, a highly influential text in probability theory.

1662

John Graunt, an English businessman and pioneer in statistics, publishes his research on the London Bills of Mortality.

1673

Gottfried Leibniz, a German philosopher and mathematician, constructs a mechanical calculator that can perform addition, subtraction, multiplication, division, and extraction of roots.

1683

Seki Kōwa, a Japanese mathematician, discovers the theory of determinants.

1684

Gottfried Leibniz publishes the first paper on calculus, *Nova Methodus pro Maximis et Minimis*.

1687

Isaac Newton, a British mathematician and physicist, publishes *Philosophiae Naturalis Principia Mathematica*, beginning a new era in science.

1693

Edmund Halley, a British mathematician and astronomer, undertakes a statistical study of the mortality rate in Breslau, Germany.

1698

Thomas Savery, an English engineer and inventor, patents the first steam engine.

1705

Jacob Bernoulli, a Swiss mathematician, dies. His major work on probability, *Ars Conjectandi*, is published in 1713.

1712

The first Newcomen steam engine is installed.

1718

Abraham de Moivre, a French mathematician, publishes *The Doctrine of Chances*, the most advanced text of the time on the theory of probability.

1743

The Anglo-Irish Anglican bishop and philosopher George Berkeley publishes *The Analyst*, an attack on the new mathematics pioneered by Isaac Newton and Gottfried Leibniz.

The French mathematician and philosopher Jean Le Rond d'Alembert begins work on the *Encyclopédie*, one of the great works of the Enlightenment.

1748

Leonhard Euler, a Swiss mathematician, publishes his *Introductio*.

1749

The French mathematician and scientist George-Louis Leclerc Buffon publishes the first volume of *Histoire naturelle*.

1750

Gabriel Cramer, a Swiss mathematician, publishes Cramer's rule, a procedure for solving systems of linear equations.

1760

Daniel Bernoulli, a Swiss mathematician and scientist, publishes his probabilistic analysis of the risks and benefits of variolation against smallpox.

1761

Thomas Bayes, an English theologian and mathematician, dies. His "Essay Towards Solving a Problem in the Doctrine of Chances" is published two years later.

The English scientist Joseph Black proposes the idea of latent heat.

1762

Catherine II (Catherine the Great) is proclaimed empress of Russia.

1769

James Watt obtains his first steam engine patent.

1775

American colonists and British troops fight battles at Lexington and Concord, Massachusetts.

1778

Voltaire (François-Marie Arouet), a French writer and philosopher, dies.

1781

William Herschel, a German-born British musician and astronomer, discovers Uranus.

1789

Unrest in France culminates in the French Revolution.

1793

The Reign of Terror, a period of brutal, state-sanctioned repression, begins in France.

1794

The French mathematician Adrien-Marie Legendre (or Le Gendre) publishes his *Éléments de géométrie*, a text that influences mathematics education for decades.

Antoine-Laurent Lavoisier, a French scientist and discoverer of the law of conservation of matter, is executed by the French government.

1798

Benjamin Thompson (Count Rumford), a British physicist, proposes the equivalence of heat and work.

1799

Napoléon seizes control of the French government.

Caspar Wessel, a Norwegian mathematician and surveyor, publishes the first geometric representation of the complex numbers.

1801

Carl Friedrich Gauss, a German mathematician, publishes *Disquisitiones Arithmeticae*.

1805

Adrien-Marie Legendre, a French mathematician, publishes "Nouvelles méthodes pour la détermination des orbites des comètes," which contains the first description of the method of least squares.

1806

Jean-Robert Argand, a French bookkeeper, accountant, and mathematician, develops the Argand diagram to represent complex numbers.

1812

Pierre-Simon Laplace, a French mathematician, publishes *Théorie analytique des probabilités*, the most influential 19th-century work on the theory of probability.

1815

Napoléon suffers final defeat at the battle of Waterloo.

Jean-Victor Poncelet, a French mathematician and "father of projective geometry," publishes *Traité des propriétés projectives des figures*.

1824

The French engineer Sadi Carnot publishes *Réflexions*, wherein he describes the Carnot engine.

Niels Henrik Abel, a Norwegian mathematician, publishes his proof of the impossibility of algebraically solving a general fifth-degree equation.

1826

Nikolai Ivanovich Lobachevsky, a Russian mathematician and "the Copernicus of geometry," announces his theory of non-Euclidean geometry.

1828

Robert Brown, a Scottish botanist, publishes the first description of Brownian motion in "A Brief Account of Microscopical Observations."

1830

Charles Babbage, a British mathematician and inventor, begins work on his analytical engine, the first attempt at a modern computer.

1832

János Bolyai, a Hungarian mathematician, publishes *Absolute Science of Space*.

The French mathematician Evariste Galois is killed in a duel.

1843

James Prescott Joule publishes his measurement of the mechanical equivalent of heat.

1846

The planet Neptune is discovered by the French mathematician Urbain-Jean-Joseph Le Verrier from a mathematical analysis of the orbit of Uranus.

1847

Georg Christian von Staudt publishes *Geometrie der Lage*, which shows that projective geometry can be expressed without any concept of length.

1848

Bernhard Bolzano, a Czech mathematician and theologian, dies. His study of infinite sets, *Paradoxien des Unendlichen*, is published in 1851.

1850

Rudolph Clausius, a German mathematician and physicist, publishes his first paper on the theory of heat.

1851

William Thomson (Lord Kelvin), a British scientist, publishes "On the Dynamical Theory of Heat."

1854

George Boole, a British mathematician, publishes *Laws of Thought*. The mathematics contained therein later makes possible the design of computer logic circuits.

The German mathematician Bernhard Riemann gives the historic lecture "On the Hypotheses That Form the Foundations of Geometry." The ideas therein later play an integral part in the theory of relativity.

1855

John Snow, a British physician, publishes "On the Mode of Communication of Cholera," the first successful epidemiological study of a disease.

1859

James Clerk Maxwell, a British physicist, proposes a probabilistic model for the distribution of molecular velocities in a gas.

Charles Darwin, a British biologist, publishes *On the Origin of Species by Means of Natural Selection*.

1861

The American Civil War begins.

1866

The Austrian biologist and monk Gregor Mendel publishes his ideas on the theory of heredity in "Versuche über Pflanzenhybriden."

1867

The Canadian Articles of Confederation unify the British colonies of North America.

1871

Otto von Bismarck is appointed first chancellor of the German Empire.

1872

The German mathematician Felix Klein announces his Erlanger Programm, an attempt to categorize all geometries with the use of group theory.

William Thomson (Lord Kelvin) develops an early analog computer to predict tides.

Richard Dedekind, a German mathematician, rigorously establishes the connection between real numbers and the real number line.

1874

Georg Cantor, a German mathematician, publishes "Über eine Eigenschaft des Inbegriffes aller reelen algebraischen Zahlen," a pioneering paper that shows that all infinite sets are not the same size.

1890

The Hollerith tabulator, an important innovation in calculating machines, is installed at the United States Census for use in the 1890 census.

1899

The German mathematician David Hilbert publishes the definitive axiomatic treatment of Euclidean geometry.

1900

David Hilbert announces his list of mathematics problems for the 20th century.

The Russian mathematician Andrey Andreyevich Markov begins his research into the theory of probability.

1901

Henri-Léon Lebesgue, a French mathematician, develops his theory of integration.

1905

Ernst Zermelo, a German mathematician, undertakes the task of axiomatizing set theory.

Albert Einstein, a German-born American physicist, begins to publish his discoveries in physics.

1906

Marian Smoluchowski, a Polish scientist, publishes his insights into Brownian motion.

1908

The Hardy-Weinberg law, containing ideas fundamental to population genetics, is published.

1910

Bertrand Russell, a British logician and philosopher, and Alfred North Whitehead, a British mathematician and philosopher, publish *Principia Mathematica*, an important work on the foundations of mathematics.

1914

World War I begins.

1917

Vladimir Ilyich Lenin leads a revolution that results in the founding of the Union of Soviet Socialist Republics.

1918

World War I ends.

The German mathematician Emmy Noether presents her ideas on the roles of symmetries in physics.

1929

Andrei Nikolayevich Kolmogorov, a Russian mathematician, publishes *General Theory of Measure and Probability Theory*, establishing the theory of probability on a firm axiomatic basis for the first time.

1930

Ronald Aylmer Fisher, a British geneticist and statistician, publishes *Genetical Theory of Natural Selection*, an important early attempt to express the theory of natural selection in mathematics.

1931

Kurt Gödel, an Austrian-born American mathematician, publishes his incompleteness proof.

The Differential Analyzer, an important development in analog computers, is developed at the Massachusetts Institute of Technology.

1933

Karl Pearson, a British innovator in statistics, retires from University College, London.

1935

George Horace Gallup, a U.S. statistician, founds the American Institute of Public Opinion.

1937

The British mathematician Alan Turing publishes his insights on the limits of computability.

1939

World War II begins.

William Edwards Deming joins the United States Census Bureau.

1945

World War II ends.

1946

The Electronic Numerical Integrator and Calculator (ENIAC) computer begins operation at the University of Pennsylvania.

1948

While working at Bell Telephone Labs in the United States, Claude Shannon publishes "A Mathematical Theory of Communication," marking the beginning of the Information Age.

1951

The Universal Automatic Computer (UNIVAC I) is installed at the U.S. Bureau of the Census.

1954

FORmula TRANslator (Fortran), one of the first high-level computer languages, is introduced.

1956

The American Walter Shewhart, an innovator in the field of quality control, retires from Bell Telephone Laboratories.

1957

Olga Oleinik publishes "Discontinuous Solutions to Nonlinear Differential Equations," a milestone in mathematical physics.

1964

IBM Corporation introduces the IBM System/360 computer for government agencies and large businesses.

1965

Andrey Nikolayevich Kolmogorov establishes the branch of mathematics now known as Kolmogorov complexity.

1966

The A Programming Language (APL) computer language is implemented on the IBM System/360 computer.

1972

Amid much fanfare, the French mathematician and philosopher René Thom establishes a new field of mathematics called catastrophe theory.

1973

The C computer language, developed at Bell Laboratories, is essentially completed.

1975

The French geophysicist Jean Morlet helps develop a new kind of analysis based on what he calls wavelets.

1977

Digital Equipment Corporation introduces the VAX computer.

1981

IBM Corporation introduces the IBM personal computer (PC).

1989

The Belgian mathematician Ingrid Daubechies develops what has become the mathematical foundation for today's wavelet research.

1991

The Union of Soviet Socialist Republics dissolves into 15 separate nations.

1995

The British mathematician Andrew Wiles publishes the first proof of Fermat's last theorem.

Cray Research introduces the CRAY E-1200, a machine that sustains a rate of 1 terraflop (1 trillion calculations per second) on real-world applications.

The JAVA computer language is introduced commercially by Sun Microsystems.

1997

René Thom declares the mathematical field of catastrophe theory "dead."

2002

Experimental Mathematics celebrates its 10th anniversary. It is a refereed journal dedicated to the experimental aspects of mathematical research.

Manindra Agrawal, Neeraj Kayal, and Nitin Saxena create a brief, elegant algorithm to test whether a number is prime, thereby solving an important centuries-old problem.

2003

Grigory Perelman produces what may be the first complete proof of the Poincaré conjecture, a statement on the most fundamental properties of three-dimensional shapes.

GLOSSARY

absolute space the belief that physical space exists independently of what it encloses

absolute time the theory that asserts that the passage of time proceeds at the same pace in all reference frames

algebra a generalization of arithmetic in which letters are used instead of numbers and combined according to the usual arithmetic procedures

analytic geometry the study of geometry by means of algebra and coordinate systems

axiom a statement accepted as true to serve as a basis for deductive reasoning. Today the words *axiom* and *postulate* are synonyms

calculus the branch of mathematics that is based on the ideas and techniques of differentiation and integration. The techniques of calculus have enabled researchers to solve many problems in mathematics and physics

Cartesian coordinates the method of establishing a one-to-one correspondence between points in *n*-dimensional space and *n*-tuples of numbers by using *n* lines that meet at a central point (the origin) at right angles to each other, where the letter *n* represents any natural number

congruence the geometric relation between figures that is analogous to "equality" in arithmetic. Two triangles are said to be congruent if they can be superimposed one on the other via a combination of translations and rotations

conic see CONIC SECTION

conic section any member of the family of curves obtained from the intersection of a double cone and a plane

coordinate system a method of establishing a one-to-one correspondence between points in space and sets of numbers

cross-ratio a property preserved by projective transformations. Let A, B, C, and D be four collinear points, listed in the order along the line in which they are positioned. Let A', B', C', and D' be their images under a projective transformation. Let AB, $C'D'$, for example, represent the directed distances between the points A and B, and C' and D', respectively. The cross-ratios, defined as $(AC/CB)/(AD/DB)$ and $(A'C'/C'B')/(A'D'/D'B')$, are always equal

deduction a conclusion obtained by logically reasoning from general principles to particular statements

derivative the limit of a ratio formed by the difference in the dependent variable to the difference in the independent variable as the difference in the independent variable tends toward 0

differential geometry that branch of geometry that uses calculus in the study of the local properties of curves and surfaces

differentiation the act of computing a derivative

duality, principle of the principle in projective geometry that asserts that every theorem about points and lines remains true when the words *point* and *line* are interchanged and the grammar adjusted accordingly

ellipse a closed curve obtained by the intersection of a right circular cone and a plane

Euclidean geometry the geometry that developed as a series of logical consequences from the axioms and postulates listed in Euclid of Alexandria's *Elements*

fifth postulate one of Euclid's statements defining the nature of the geometry that he studied. It asserts, in effect, that given a line and a point not on the line, exactly one line can be drawn through the given point that is parallel to the given line

fundamental principle of analytic geometry the observation that under fairly general conditions one equation in two variables defines a curve

fundamental principle of solid analytic geometry the observation that under fairly general conditions one equation in three variables defines a surface

geodesic the shortest path between two points lying in a given surface

geometric algebra a method of expressing ideas usually associated with algebra by using the concepts and techniques of Euclidean geometry

group a set of objects together with an operation analogous to multiplication such that (1) the "product" of any two elements in the set is an element in the set; (2) the operation is associative, that is, for any three elements, a, b, and c, in the group $(ab)c = a(bc)$; (3) there is an element in the set, usually denoted with the letter e, such that $ea = ae = a$, where a is any element in the set; and (4) every element in the set has an inverse, so that if a is an element in the set, there is an element called a^{-1} such that $aa^{-1} = e$

hexagon a polygon with six angles and six sides

Hilbert space a type of mathematical space named after the mathematician David Hilbert (1862–1943). Hilbert spaces are usually infinite dimensional and are generally used in the study of sets of functions

hyperbola a curve composed of the intersection of a plane and both parts of a double right circular cone

indeterminate equation an equation or set of equations for which there exist infinitely many solutions

integration the ideas and techniques belonging to calculus that are used in computing the lengths of curves, the size of areas, and the volumes of solids

invariant unchanged by a particular set of mathematical or physical transformations

method of exhaustion the proposition in Greek geometry that given any magnitude M one can, by continually reducing its size by at least half, make the magnitude as small as desired. Given a "small" positive number, usually denoted by the Greek letter ε (epsilon), and a number r such that $0 < r < 1/2$, then $M \times r^n < \varepsilon$ provided that n is a sufficiently large natural number. This proposition formed the basis for the Greek analog to calculus

parabola the curve formed by the intersection of a right circular cone and a plane that is parallel to a line that generates the cone

perspective the process of representing on a planar surface the spatial relations of three-dimensional objects as they appear to the eye

point at infinity in projective geometry the point at infinity is analogous to the *vanishing point* in representational art. It is the point of intersection of two "parallel" lines

postulate see AXIOM

projection in projective geometry, a transformation of an image or object that maintains a sense of perspective

projective geometry the branch of geometry concerned with the properties of figures that are invariant under projections

Pythagorean theorem the statement that for a right triangle the square of the length of the hypotenuse equals the sum of the squares of the lengths of the remaining sides

Pythagorean triple three numbers, each of which is a natural number, such that the sum of the squares of the two smaller numbers equals the square of the largest number

quadric surface any surface described by a second-degree equation in the variables x, y, and z. There are six quadric surfaces: ellipsoid, hyperboloid of one sheet, hyperboloid of two sheets, elliptic cone, elliptic paraboloid, and hyperbolic paraboloid

reference frame a system of lines that are imagined to be attached to a point called the *origin* and that serve to identify the position of any other point in space in relation to the origin

set a collection of objects or symbols

special relativity a physical theory based on the assertion that the laws of physics—including the speed of light—are the same in all frames of reference in uniform motion

solid analytic geometry the branch of analytic geometry that is principally concerned with the properties of surfaces

synthetic geometry geometry that is expressed without the use of algebraic or analytic symbols

tangent the best straight-line approximation to a smoothly varying curve at a given point

transformation the act or process of mapping one geometrical object onto another such that it establishes a one-to-one correspondence between the points of the object and its image

FURTHER READING

MODERN WORKS

Abbot, Edwin A. *Flatland: A Romance of Many Dimensions.* New York: New American Library, 1984. This novel about the mathematical concept of spatial dimensions has kept mathematically inclined readers entertained for decades.

Boles, Martha, and Rochelle Newman. *Universal Patterns: The Golden Relationship: Art, Math and Nature.* Bradford, Mass.: Pythagorean Press, 1990. A combination of art, math, and an introduction to the straightedge and compass techniques required to construct many basic figures, this book is unique and very accessible.

Boyer, Carl B., and Uta C. Merzbach. *A History of Mathematics.* New York: John Wiley & Sons, 1991. Boyer was one of the preeminent mathematics historians of the 20th century. This work contains much interesting biographical information. The mathematical information assumes a fairly strong background of the reader.

Bruno, Leonard C. *Math and Mathematicians: The History of Mathematics Discoveries around the World,* 2 vols. Detroit, Mich.: U.X.L, 1999. Despite its name there is little mathematics in this two-volume set. What you will find is a very large number of brief biographies of many individuals who were important in the history of mathematics.

Bunt, Lucas Nicolaas Hendrik, Phillip S. Jones, Jack D. Bedient. *The Historical Roots of Elementary Mathematics.* Englewood Cliffs, N.J.: Prentice Hall, 1976. A highly detailed examination—complete with numerous exercises—of how ancient cultures added, subtracted, divided, multiplied, and reasoned.

Courant, Richard, and Herbert Robbins. *What Is Mathematics? An Elementary Approach to Ideas and Mathematics.* New York: Oxford University Press, 1941. A classic and exhaustive answer to the question posed in the title. Courant was an influential 20th-century mathematician.

Dewdney, Alexander K. *200% of Nothing: An Eye-Opening Tour through the Twists and Turns of Math Abuse and Innumeracy.* New York: John Wiley & Sons, 1993. A critical look at ways mathematical reasoning has been abused to distort truth.

Diggins, Julia D. *Strings, Straightedge and Shadow: The Story of Geometry.* New York: Viking Press, 1965. Greek geometry for young readers.

Durell, Clement V. "The Theory of Relativity." In *The World of Mathematics.* Vol. 3, edited by James R. Newman. New York: Dover Publications, 1956. This article is a careful exposition of some of the more peculiar geometric consequences of the theory of relativity. Very well written.

Eastaway, Robert, and Jeremy Wyndham. *Why Do Buses Come in Threes? The Hidden Mathematics of Everyday Life.* New York: John Wiley & Sons, 1998. Nineteen lighthearted essays on the mathematics underlying everything from luck to scheduling problems.

Eves, Howard. *An Introduction to the History of Mathematics.* New York: Holt, Rinehart & Winston, 1953. This well-written history of mathematics places special emphasis on early mathematics. It is unusual because the history is accompanied by numerous mathematical problems. (The solutions are in the back of the book.)

Field, Judith V. *The Invention of Infinity: Mathematics and Art in the Renaissance.* New York: Oxford University Press, 1997. This is a beautiful, very detailed story of the development of representational art and the beginnings of projective geometry. The text is accompanied by many drawings and pictures.

Freudenthal, Hans. *Mathematics Observed.* New York: McGraw-Hill, 1967. A collection of seven survey articles about math topics from computability to geometry to physics (some more technical than others).

Gardner, Martin. *The Ambidextrous Universe: Mirror Asymmetry and Time-Reversed Worlds.* New York: Scribner, 1979. A readable look at geometric transformations and their meaning.

————. *The Colossal Book of Mathematics.* New York: Norton, 2001. Martin Gardner had a gift for seeing things mathematically. This "colossal" book contains sections on geometry, algebra, probability, logic, and more.

Ghyka, Matila. *The Geometry of Art and Life.* New York: Dover Publications, 1977. An exploration of geometric ideas as they appear in the world around us with special emphasis on geometry as it was known to Euclid.

Guillen, Michael. *Bridges to Infinity: The Human Side of Mathematics.* Los Angeles: Jeremy P. Tarcher, 1983. This book consists of an engaging nontechnical set of essays on mathematical topics, including non-Euclidean geometry, transfinite numbers, and catastrophe theory.

Heath, Thomas L. *A History of Greek Mathematics.* New York: Dover Publications, 1981. First published early in the 20th century and reprinted numerous times, this book is still one of the main references on the subject.

Hoffman, Paul. *Archimedes' Revenge: The Joys and Perils of Mathematics.* New York: Ballantine, 1989. A relaxed, sometimes silly look at an interesting and diverse set of math topics ranging from prime numbers and cryptography to Turing machines and the mathematics of democratic processes.

Joseph, George G. *The Crest of the Peacock: The Non-European Roots of Mathematics.* Princeton, N.J.: Princeton University Press, 1991. One of the best of a new crop of books devoted to this important topic.

Kline, Morris. *Mathematics and the Physical World.* New York: Thomas Y. Crowell, 1959. The history of mathematics as it relates to the history of science, and vice versa.

————. *Mathematics for the Nonmathematician.* New York: Dover Publications, 1985. An articulate, not very technical overview of many important mathematical ideas.

————. *Mathematics in Western Culture.* New York: Oxford University Press, 1953. An excellent overview of the development of Western mathematics in its cultural context, this book is aimed at an audience with a firm grasp of high school–level mathematics.

————. "Projective Geometry." In *The World of Mathematics*. Vol. 1, edited by James R. Newman. New York: Dover Publications, 1956. This is an excellent introduction to projective geometry accompanied by many skillful illustrations. Though not especially easy to read, it is well worth the time.

Mlodinow, Leonard. *Euclid's Window: The Story of Geometry from Parallel Lines to Hyperspace*. New York: The Free Press, 2001. An interesting narrative about the interplay between geometry and our views of the universe from Thales to the present.

Pappas, Theoni. *The Joy of Mathematics*. San Carlos, Calif.: World Wide/Tetra, 1986. Aimed at a younger audience, this work searches for interesting applications of mathematics in the world around us.

Ruchlis, Hy, and Jack Englehardt. *The Story of Mathematics: Geometry for the Young Scientist*. Irvington-on-Hudson, N.Y.: Harvey House, 1958. A clever survey of geometry in our lives.

Rucker, Rudy. *The Fourth Dimension: Toward a Geometry of Higher Reality*. Boston: Houghton Mifflin, 1984. An interesting examination of ideas associated with geometry and perception.

Sawyer, Walter. *What Is Calculus About?* New York: Random House, 1961. A highly readable description of a sometimes-intimidating, historically important subject. Absolutely no calculus background required.

Schiffer, M., and Leon Bowden. *The Role of Mathematics in Science*. Washington, D.C.: Mathematical Association of America, 1984. The first few chapters of this book, ostensibly written for high school students, will be accessible to many students; the last few chapters will find a much narrower audience.

Smith, David E., and Yoshio Mikami. *A History of Japanese Mathematics*. Chicago: The Open Court Publishing Co., 1914. Copies of this book are still around, and it is frequently quoted. The first half is an informative nontechnical survey. The second half is written more for the expert.

Stewart, Ian. *From Here to Infinity*. New York: Oxford University Press, 1996. A well-written, very readable overview of several important contemporary ideas in geometry, algebra, computability, chaos, and mathematics in nature.

Swetz, Frank J., editor. *From Five Fingers to Infinity: A Journey through the History of Mathematics*. Chicago: Open Court, 1994. This is a fascinating though not especially focused look at the history of mathematics.

————. *Sea Island Mathematical Manual: Surveying and Mathematics in Ancient China*. University Park: The Pennsylvania State University Press, 1992. The book contains many ancient problems in mathematics and measurement and illustrates how problems in measurement often inspired the development of geometric ideas and techniques.

————, and T. I. Kao. *Was Pythagoras Chinese? An Examination of Right Triangle Theory in Ancient China*. University Park: The Pennsylvania State University Press, and Reston, Va.: National Council of Teachers of Mathematics, 1977. Inspired by the book of Smith and Mikami (also listed in this bibliography), the authors examine numerous ancient Chinese problems involving right triangles while providing helpful commentary.

Tabak, John. *Mathematics and the Laws of Nature: Developing the Language of Science*. New York: Facts On File, 2004. More information about the relationships that exist between math and the laws of nature.

Thomas, David A. *Math Projects for Young Scientists*. New York: Franklin Watts, 1988. This project-oriented text gives an introduction to several historically important geometry problems.

Yaglom, Isaac M. *Geometric Transformations*, translated by Allen Shields. New York: Random House, 1962. Aimed at high school students, this is a very sophisticated treatment of "simple" geometry and an excellent introduction to higher mathematics. It is also an excellent introduction to the concept of invariance.

Yoler, Yusuf A. *Perception of Natural Events by Human Observers*. Bellevue, Wash.: Unipress, 1993. Sections one and three of this book give a nice overview of the geometry that is a consequence of the theory of relativity.

ORIGINAL SOURCES

It can sometimes deepen our appreciation of an important mathematical discovery to read the discoverer's own description. Often this is not possible, because the description is too technical. Fortunately there are exceptions. Sometimes the discovery is accessible because the idea does not require a lot of technical background to be appreciated. Sometimes the discoverer writes a nontechnical account of the technical idea that she or he has discovered. Here are some classic papers:

Ahmes. *The Rhind Mathematical Papyrus: Free Translation, Commentary, and Selected Photographs, Transcription, Literal Translations*, translated by Arnold B. Chace. Reston, Va.: National Council of Teachers of Mathematics, 1979. This is a translation of the biggest and best of extant Egyptian mathematical texts, the Rhind papyrus (also known as the Ahmes papyrus). It provides insight into the types of problems and methods of solution known to one of humanity's oldest cultures.

Descartes, René. *The Geometry.* In *The World of Mathematics.* Vol. 1, edited by James Newman. New York: Dover Publications, 1956. This is a readable translation of an excerpt from Descartes's own revolutionary work *La Géométrie*.

Dürer, Albrecht. *The Human Figure by Albrecht Dürer*, edited and translated by Walter L. Strauss. New York: Dover Publications, 1972. This is a large collection of sketches by the famous artist. The sketches, especially those in the second half of the book, clearly show Dürer's searching for connections between his art and what would later be known as projective geometry.

Euclid of Alexandria. *Elements.* Translated by Sir Thomas L. Heath. *Great Books of the Western World.* Vol. 11. Chicago: Encyclopaedia Britannica, 1952. See especially *Book I* for Euclid's own exposition of the axiomatic method and read some of the early propositions in this volume to see how the Greeks investigated mathematics without equations.

Galilei, Galileo. *Dialogues Concerning Two New Sciences*, translated by Henry Crew and Alfonso de Salvio. New York: Dover Publications,

1954. An interesting literary work as well as a pioneering physics text. Many regard the publication of this text as the beginning of the modern scientific tradition. The chapter "Fourth Day" shows how parabolas and the geometry of Apollonius were used to describe projectile motion.

Hardy, Godfrey H. *A Mathematician's Apology*. Cambridge, England: Cambridge University Press, 1940. Hardy was an excellent mathematician and a good writer. In this oft-quoted and very brief book Hardy seeks to explain and sometimes justify his life as a mathematician.

Weyl, Hermann. Symmetry. In *World of Mathematics*. Vol. 1, edited by James R. Newman. New York: Dover Publications, 1956. An extended meditation on a geometric idea that has become a central organizing principle in contemporary physics by a pioneer in the subject.

INTERNET RESOURCES

Athena Earth and Space Science for K–12. Available on-line. URL: http://inspire.ospi.wednet.edu:8001/. Updated May 13, 1999. Funded by the National Aeronautics and Space Administration's (NASA's) Public Use of Remote Sensing Data, this site contains many interesting applications of mathematics to the study of natural phenomena.

Electronic Bookshelf. Available on-line. URL: http://hilbert.dartmouth.cdu/~matc/eBookshelf/art/index.html. Updated on May 21, 2002. This site is maintained by Dartmouth College. It is both visually beautiful and informative, and it has links to many creative presentations on computer science, the history of mathematics, and mathematics. It also treats a number of other topics from a mathematical perspective.

Eric Weisstein's World of Mathematics. Available on-line. URL: http://mathworld.wolfram.com/. Updated on April 10, 2002. This site has brief overviews of a great many topics in mathematics. The level of presentation varies substantially from topic to topic.

Faber, Vance, Bonnie Yantis, Mike Hawrylycz, Nancy Casey, Mike Fellows, Mike Barnett, Gretchen Wissner. This is MEGA

Mathematics! Available on-line. URL: http://www.c3.lanl.gov/ mega-math. Updated June 2, 2003. Maintained by the Los Alamos National Laboratories, one of the premier scientific establishments in the world, this site has a number of unusual offerings. It is well worth a visit.

Fife, Earl, and Larry Husch. Math Archives. "History of Mathematics." Available on-line. URL: http://archives.math. utk.edu/topics/history.html. Updated January 2002. Information on mathematics, mathematicians, and mathematical organizations.

Gangolli, Ramesh. *Asian Contributions to Mathematics.* Available on-line. URL: http://www.pps.k12.or.us/depts-c/mc-me/be-as-ma.pdf. Updated on June 2, 2003. As its name implies, this well-written on-line book focuses on the history of mathematics in Asia and its effect on the world history of mathematics. It also includes information on the work of Asian Americans, a welcome contribution to the field.

Howard, Mike. *Introduction to Crystallography and Mineral Crystal Systems.* Available on-line. URL: http://www.rockhounds.com/ rockshop/xtal/. Downloaded June 3, 2003. The author has designed a nice introduction to the use of group theory in the study of crystals through an interesting mix of geometry, algebra, and mineralogy.

The Math Forum @ Drexel. The Math Forum Student Center. Available on-line. URL: http://mathforum.org/students/. Updated June 2, 2003. Probably the best website for information about the kinds of mathematics that students encounter in their school-related studies. You will find interesting and challenging problems and solutions for students in grades K–12 as well as a fair amount of college-level information.

Melville, Duncan J. Mesopotamian Mathematics. Available on-line. URL: http://it.stlawu.edu/ca.dmelvill/mesomath/. Updated March 17, 2003. This creative site is devoted to many aspects of Mesopotamian mathematics. It also has a link to a "cuneiform calculator," which can be fun to use.

O'Connor, John L., and Edmund F. Robertson. The MacTutor History of Mathematics Archive. Available on-line. URL: http://www.gap.dcs.st-and.ac.uk/~history/index.html. Updated

May 2003. This is a valuable resource for anyone interested in learning more about the history of mathematics. It contains an extraordinary collection of biographies of mathematicians of different cultures and times. In addition it provides information about the historical development of certain key mathematical ideas.

PERIODICALS, THROUGH THE MAIL AND ON-LINE

+Plus

URL: http://pass.maths.org.uk
A site with numerous interesting articles about all aspects of high school math. They send an email every few weeks to their subscribers to keep them informed about new articles at the site.

Function

Business Manager
Department of Mathematics and Statistics
Monash University
Victoria 3800
Australia
function@maths.monash.edu.au
Published five times per year, this refereed journal is aimed at older high school students.

The Math Goodies Newsletter

http://www.mathgoodies.com/newsletter/
A popular, free e-newsletter that is sent out twice per month.

Parabola: A Mathematics Magazine for Secondary Students

Australian Mathematics Trust
University of Canberra
ACT 2601
Australia

Published twice a year by the Australian Mathematics Trust in association with the University of New South Wales, *Parabola* is a source of short high-quality articles on many aspects of mathematics. Some back issues are also available free on-line. See URL: http://www.maths.unsw.edu.au/Parabola/index.html.

Pi in the Sky

http://www.pims.math.ca/pi/
Part of the Pacific Institute for the Mathematical Sciences, this high school mathematics magazine is available over the Internet.

Scientific American

415 Madison Avenue
New York, NY 10017
A serious and widely read monthly magazine, *Scientific American* regularly carries high-quality articles on mathematics and mathematically intensive branches of science. This is the one "popular" source of high-quality mathematical information that you will find at a newsstand.

INDEX

Italic page numbers indicate illustrations.

A

Abel, Niels Henrik 86
Absolute Science of Space
(Bolyai) 97–98
absolute space and time,
Newton on 127–128,
156
abstraction, algebraic notation and 102
Académie des Sciences
(Paris), Monge at 77
Ahmes papyrus 5–6
Alberti, Leon Battista 58
alchemy, Newton's interest
in 124
Alexandria (Egypt)
Euclid in 24
Greek mathematicians
educated in 19–20, 32,
39
learning and scholarship
in 48
Pappus in 43
algebra
fundamental theorem of
99
geometric, in Euclid's
Elements 26
geometric interpreta-
tions of 110
and geometry
conceptual bridge
between 103
study of 102
Greek disinterest in 15,
36, 42, 106
Hindu 52–53
Islamic 49, 54
Mesopotamian 7
analysis
discovery of field of 75
functional 170
global 140
importance of 144

local 140
use of geometric meth-
ods in, Monge and 77
analytic geometry
102–139
as applied mathematics
139
and calculus 120
definition of 102
Descartes and 108,
110–114
Euler and 130–137
Fermat and 116
fundamental principle of
Descartes on 113
Fermat on 116
Gergonne and 84
and graphing 113
importance of 102
Monge and 138
Newton and 125
solid 130–133
angle(s)
in projective geometry
67
trisection of
Archimedes on 36
classical Greek prob-
lem of 20
Pappus on 44–45
Annales de Gergonne (journal) 83
Apollonius of Perga
37–39, 106–107
Conics 39–43, 107
Hypatia's commentary
on 48
Pappus's commentary
on 44
theorem from 112
title page of 18th-cen-
tury edition *38*
coordinate system of
107–108

Cutting-off of a Ratio 39
Plane Loci 115
*Applications of Analysis and
Geometry* (Poncelet) 80
approximation 4
Mesopotamian use of 7,
8
Archimedes of Syracuse
19, 32–37
death of 34
grave of 35
The Method 34, 37
page of essay by *33*
*Quadrature of the
Parabola* 36
on semiregular solids 44
*On the Sphere and
Cylinder* 34, *35*
On Spirals 35–36
Pappus's commentary
on 44
writing style of 36–37
architecture
Egyptian *4, 5*
Greek *11*
golden section in 17,
19
Archytas of Tarentum 21,
22
area
Archimedes on compu-
tation of 36
of circle, Egyptian for-
mula for 4
of isosceles triangle,
Egyptian computation
of 5–6, *6*
of triangle 6
Aristarchus of Samos 34
Arithmetica (Diophantus),
Hypatia's commentary on
48
Arithmetica Universalis
(Newton) 125

X